Remembering the
the
Pennsylvania
Railroad

Above: Restored Pennsylvania Railroad 2,250 horsepower type E8A diesel locomotives No. 5711 (built in October 1952 later Penn Central No. 4311, Amtrak No. 317, Amtrak No. 499, and Conrail No. 4021) and No. 5809 (built in January 1951 later Penn Central No. 4309, Amtrak No. 315, Amtrak No. 498, Conrail No. 4020, and Norfolk Southern Railway No. 1000) are on a special excursion that stopped at Jamestown, New York on August 6, 2011. There were seventy-four of these locomotives built by the Electro-Motive Division of General Motors Corporation for the Pennsylvania Railroad. (*Photograph by Kenneth C. Springirth*)

On the Cover: Vintage Pennsylvania Railroad class I1sa steam locomotive No. 4483 Decapod type steam locomotive with a 2-10-0 wheel arrangement has been preserved by the Western New York Railway Historical Society and is shown at their Hamburg, New York site on June 25, 2013. This locomotive was built by the Baldwin Locomotive Works in May 1923. The Pennsylvania Railroad had 598 of these locomotives, and they were successfully used for slow drag service. (*Photograph by Kenneth C. Springirth*)

Remembering

THE

Pennsylvania Railroad

Kenneth C. Springirth

AMERICA
THROUGH TIME®
ADDING COLOR TO AMERICAN HISTORY

This 570 horsepower class BB1 switcher type electric locomotive No. 3900 with a 0-6-0 wheel arrangement is moving passenger cars in this 1926 view. The locomotive, weighing 157,045 pounds, was built at the Pennsylvania Railroad's Juniata Shops at Altoona in October 1926 and was scrapped in December 1962. Motors and controls were supplied by Westinghouse Electric and Manufacturing Company. Two of these locomotives could be coupled together and operated by one crew. Between 1926 and 1935, there were forty-two of these locomotives built and used in the New York Terminal District between Sunnyside Yard and Penn Station in New York, in Philadelphia between Penn Coach yard and 30th Street Station in Philadelphia, and a few units were used at the Pennsylvania Railroad Harrisburg station. As passenger traffic decreased in the 1950s and 1960s, the need for dedicated electric switchers decreased, and all were scrapped except for one unit preserved at the Railroad Museum of Pennsylvania.

AMERICA THROUGH TIME® is an imprint of Fonthill Media LLC
www.through-time.com
office@through-time.com

Published by Arcadia Publishing by arrangement with Fonthill Media LLC
For all general information, please contact Arcadia Publishing:
Telephone: 843-853-2070   Fax: 843-853-0044
E-mail: sales@arcadiapublishing.com
For customer service and orders:
Toll-Free 1-888-313-2665

www.arcadiapublishing.com

First published in the United States of America 2013. Reprinted 2018.
First published in the United Kingdom 2014. Reprinted 2018.

Copyright © Kenneth C. Springirth 2013, 2018

ISBN 978-1-62545-071-5

Typeset in 10pt on 13pt Palatino Nova
Printed and bound in England

CONTENTS

Acknowledgments 6

Introduction 7

Chapter 1 Freight Service 11

Chapter 2 Passenger Service 41

Chapter 3 Railroads Serving the Former Pennsylvania Railroad 85

ACKNOWLEDGMENTS

Thanks to the restoration work by Scott Symans and his friends on Viscose No. 6 locomotive has resulted in introducing the steam locomotive to a new generation with the series of railroad excursions that have been held on number of railroads. The Erie County Public Library system with its excellent staff and the Heritage room in the Blasco Memorial Library where files of the *Erie Dispatch* newspaper were reviewed. Photographs were from Darwin F. Simonaitis; Edwin Wilde; the William C. Mowris collection; Robert Feddersen and the Robert Feddersen collection; Craig Knox and the Craig Knox collection; Michael B. Shannon; Donald A. Woshlo, Jr.; Regis F. Daly; and James A. Gillin.

This is a classic builder's photograph of Pennsylvania Railroad class L5 electric locomotive No. 3930 with a 2-4-4-2 wheel arrangement around 1924. The locomotive, weighing 408,600 pounds, was built at the Pennsylvania Railroad's Juniata Shops at Altoona in January 1924 and was scrapped in May 1944. Motors and controls were supplied by Westinghouse Electric and Manufacturing Company. There were twenty-five of these locomotives built. General Electric Company and Brown Boveri each supplied motors and controls for six locomotives.

INTRODUCTION

Colonel John Stevens of Hoboken, New Jersey (who was involved with ferry operations in New York City and Philadelphia) published in 1812 *Superior Advantages of Railways and Steam Carriages over Canal Navigation* followed in 1818 by *Expediency of a Railroad from Philadelphia to Pittsburgh*. Colonel Stevens's request of December 1822 to build a railroad from Philadelphia to Columbia resulted in an Act approved March 31, 1823 to build a line from Philadelphia to Columbia, but it was not possible to secure financial support for the project. A state funded project was approved on March 24, 1828, and the first section of the Philadelphia and Columbia Railroad opened from Philadelphia to what is today Malvern on September 20, 1832 with the entire double track line opened on October 7, 1834. Johnstown, Pennsylvania was connected to Pittsburgh by the Western Division Canal in 1830. Early in 1832, the Pennsylvania Canal was completed from Columbia to Hollidaysburg. The first part of what later became the Pennsylvania Railroad was the Philadelphia and Columbia Railroad, which opened from Philadelphia to Columbia on October 7, 1834. The Allegheny Portage Railroad, an incline plane railroad connecting Hollidaysburg with Johnstown, was opened to the public on March 18, 1834.

On April 3, 1837, a charter was signed to incorporate the Sunbury and Erie Railroad in Pennsylvania, but this railroad did not get built right away because of the economic depression in the United States, sparse population in North Central and Northwestern Pennsylvania, and the inhabitants in the region did not have the construction funds. Ground breaking ceremony for the line took place on June 3, 1851 near Farrandsville, Clinton County, Pennsylvania. In 1853, the route was resurveyed and grading the line began between Milton and Williamsport, Pennsylvania. On December 18, 1854, the Sunbury and Erie Railroad was opened between Milton and Williamsport with a special train arriving at Williamsport with 300 people from Philadelphia to celebrate the event. The railroad was completed between Milton and Northumberland on September 24, 1855, was completed to Sunbury on January 6, 1856, and was opened to Lock Haven on July 1, 1859. At the western end, the line was completed from Erie to Warren, Pennsylvania on December 10, 1859. A special train arrived in Warren from Erie on December 15, 1859 at 1 p.m. and a parade was held to celebrate the arrival of the railroad to Warren. On March 7, 1861, the Sunbury and Erie Railroad became the Philadelphia and Erie Railroad. Beginning January 1, 1862, the Pennsylvania Railroad leased the Philadelphia and Erie Railroad. On January 5, 1863, the line was completed from Warren twelve miles east to Sheffield, Pennsylvania. By January 1, 1864, the eastern part of the line was completed from Sunbury to St Marys. The railroad was completed from St Marys to Emporium on May 2, 1864 and from Sheffield to Kane on May 23, 1864. Before the end of July 1864 the eastern and western construction crews met at Tambine, a small community about two miles east of Wilcox, and drove in the silver spike. On Tuesday morning October 4, 1864, a special excursion train left Philadelphia and arrived in Lock Haven that evening. The next morning it left Lock Haven and arrived in Erie Wednesday evening October 5, 1864 with about 300 passengers to celebrate the completion of the railroad from Philadelphia to Erie. "All hail to the iron band which now joins Erie with Philadelphia and the seaboard." was noted by the October 6, 1864 *Erie Dispatch* newspaper which marked yesterday's arrival of the train from Philadelphia as Erie's 'Event of greater importance than any which has hitherto transpired.' Regular passenger service began from Erie to Philadelphia on October 17, 1864, and the last run was made on March 27, 1965. On March 12,

1907, Pennsylvania Railroad stockholders approved the acquisition of the Philadelphia and Erie Railroad. In 1982, Consolidated Rail Corporation ended service west of St Marys to Erie but retained a section between Union City and Corry accessed by the former Erie Railroad. Hammermill Paper Company purchased the line and the newly organized Allegheny Railroad operated its first train on September 3, 1985. The Allegheny Railroad was acquired by the Genesee and Wyoming in 1992 becoming the Allegheny and Eastern and later became part of the Buffalo and Pittsburgh Railroad.

An 1835 Philadelphia to Pittsburgh trip required four days with eighty-two miles by train from Philadelphia to Columbia, then 172 miles by canal boat to Hollidaysburg, then 36 miles by the Allegheny Portage Railroad to Johnstown, and 104 miles by canal via the Conemaugh and Allegheny Rivers to Pittsburgh. Making the changes of conveyances was time consuming, and the service did not operate in the winter time. On April 13, 1846, the Pennsylvania Railroad received the charter authorizing construction of a railroad from Harrisburg to Pittsburgh with construction beginning in 1847. The first 60.7 miles of line from Harrisburg to Lewistown went into service on September 1, 1849 with one round trip passenger train daily. The line was opened to McVeytown, 72 miles from Harrisburg, on December 24, 1849, to Shaeffer's Aqueduct near Mount Union, 85 miles from Harrisburg, on April 1, 1850, to Huntingdon, 97 miles from Harrisburg, on June 10, 1850, and to the Portage (Hollidaysburg), 137 miles from Harrisburg, on September 16, 1850. The connection with the Portage Railroad was not in place until November 1, 1850. On December 10, 1852, service was in place from Philadelphia to Pittsburgh using the Allegheny Portage Railroad between Hollidaysburg and Johnstown. About five-and-a-half miles west of Altoona, it was decided to build a semicircle of track through the summit of the Allegheny Mountains. This became known as the Horseshoe Curve, which added almost two miles to the line but achieved a 1.75 gradient. The Horseshoe Curve section opened on February 15, 1854. As of January 1, 1856, the railroad was completed from Harrisburg to Pittsburgh, and its major purpose was to save the trade of the west for Pennsylvania and Philadelphia against the Erie Canal. On August 1, 1857, the state-owned system (including the Portage Railroad, canals, and railroad rolling stock) was purchased by the Pennsylvania Railroad for $7.5 million.

The Allegheny Valley Railroad was opened from Pittsburgh to Kittanning, Pennsylvania on January 30, 1856, opened to Templeton Station on May 2, 1866, opened to Brady's Bend on June 27, 1867, and opened to Oil City on January 8, 1868. It was leased to the Pennsylvania Railroad on July 31, 1900. Railroad lines between Buffalo and Oil City became part of the Western New York and Pennsylvania Railroad which was leased by the Pennsylvania Railroad on July 31, 1900 and later became part of the Pennsylvania Railroad's Buffalo Division.

By February 1869, the Pennsylvania Railroad had its own line from Pittsburgh to Indianapolis plus Columbus to Chicago through the leasing of the Columbus, Chicago and Indiana Central Railroad. On June 7, 1869 the Pennsylvania Railroad leased the Pittsburgh, Fort Wayne and Chicago Railroad. Beginning in 1863, the Pennsylvania Railroad gained control of 356 miles of railroad lines in New Jersey. On May 4, 1896, Pennsylvania Railroad properties in southern New Jersey were consolidated into the West Jersey and Seashore Railroad. Effective April 1, 1889, the Reading Company properties in southern New Jersey were consolidated into the Atlantic City Railroad. On June 25, 1933 the Atlantic City Railroad and the West Jersey and Seashore Railroad (which duplicated each other) were consolidated into the Pennsylvania–Reading Seashore Lines with passenger service replaced by buses on July 1, 1982. The Erie and Pittsburgh Railroad, incorporated during 1858, was opened from Girard Junction (sixteen-and-a-half miles west of Erie, Pennsylvania) to New Castle, Pennsylvania in 1864 and was leased by the Pennsylvania Railroad on March 1, 1870. The Ashtabula, Youngstown and Pittsburgh Railroad was leased by the Pennsylvania Railroad beginning January 1, 1873 and completed from Youngstown to Ashtabula Harbor, Ohio on May 1, 1873. Both of these lines provided access to docks on Lake Erie, which were important to the Pennsylvania Railroad's growing coal and ore business. In 1870, the Pennsylvania Railroad leased the Northwestern Ohio Railway Company giving it access to Toledo, Ohio. With the discovery of Oil at Titusville in 1859, by 1865 the Oil Creek Railroad linking Corry with Titusville came under Pennsylvania Railroad control.

Railroad employee wages were cut 10 percent in 1873. After the Pennsylvania Railroad cut wages 10 percent the second time throughout the system, on July 19, 1877 train crews at Pittsburgh went on strike destroying thirty-nine buildings including Union Station and destroying entire trains.

The Pennsylvania Railroad pioneered in using the Janney automatic coupler in 1882. During 1883, the Railroad acquired control of the Camden and Atlantic Railroad which connected Camden, New Jersey with Atlantic City, and electric operation began on this line on September 18, 1906. Through service from New York to Atlantic City began during 1890.

On May 31, 1889, the dam on the Conemaugh River north of Johnstown broke releasing a wall of water twenty feet high that destroyed everything in its path and resulted in the deaths of 3,000 people. More than 1,600 homes along with many shops and factories were destroyed. The railroad lost ten miles of track, 34 locomotives, 24 passenger cars and 561 freight cars. Passenger service was restored on June 24, 1889, and freight service was restored on July 17, 1889.

The 45-mile Trenton cutoff opened in 1892 from Glen Loch west of Philadelphia to Trenton, New Jersey providing a bypass for freight traffic between New York and the west. The growth of the Delmarva Peninsula (Delaware, Maryland, & Virginia) in farming and seafood resulted in the building of the New York, Philadelphia, and Norfolk Railroad which was completed during 1884 and become part of the Pennsylvania Railroad in the 1920s. The Long Island Railroad became part of the Pennsylvania Railroad during 1900.

The present stone arch bridge at Rockville, Pennsylvania was completed in April 1902 replacing the iron truss bridge that was erected in 1877, which in itself had replaced the first structure completed in 1849.

In 1917, the Pennsylvania Railroad leased the Philadelphia, Baltimore and Washington Railroad. During the First World War on December 28, 1917, the United States government took over the railroads, and the railroads were returned to their owners on March 1, 1920. Pennsylvania Railroad passenger service reached Detroit during 1920 and freight service in 1922.

Railroads performed in an outstanding manner during the Second World War by cooperating with each other plus government-owned warehouses were in place so that freight cars would not become wheeled storage sheds.

Before the the Second World War, the peak day travel on the Philadelphia–Washington line had been 68,000 passengers, and this was recorded on the day of President Roosevelt's second inaugural in 1937. By December 24, 1943, this had increased to over 178,000, recorded through the tickets collected. In 1946, the railroad suffered its first loss in 100 years. The federal government had ordered wage increases, but there was a delay in granting rate increases. Operating revenues were $867 million while operating expenses were $876 million. The railroad earned a small profit during 1947.

The railroad built many of its own steam locomotives. When it purchased locomotives, it generally provided the design specs. It standardized its fleet becoming known as the 'Standard Railroad of America'. This was later changed to the 'Standard Railroad of the World.' The standardization was internal. Passenger trains moved behind a fleet of K4 class Pacifics. The railroad had hundreds of P70 class coaches built to a single design. While many railroads used what was available, the Pennsylvania Railroad tested and experimented with equipment designs. When the right design was found, it became the company standard. The railroad preferred 'tried and true' models but experimented with new models which led to improvements in its locomotives. Colors and paint schemes were standardized. Locomotives were painted in a shade of green so dark that it looked almost black. Passenger cars were painted Tuscan red. Some electric locomotives and most diesels were painted Tuscan red. Freight cars were painted an iron oxide shade of red. On passenger locomotives and cars, the lettering and outlining was done in real gold leaf. After the Second World War, the lettering was done in a light shade of yellow called 'Buff Yellow'.

The Pennsylvania Railroad was one of the first American railroads to adopt the use of iron instead of wooden bridges. Most of the bridges on the Altoona to Pittsburgh segment of the railroad were iron when the railroad first opened in 1854, and over the next several years the railroad replaced the few remaining wooden bridges with iron ones. The railroad introduced a baggage tag system whereby a metal disc was attached to passenger luggage and a duplicate of this metal tag was given to the customer. The baggage system of cardboard tags used today evolved from that system.

In 1858, the Pennsylvania Railroad designated that all of their car shops use standard patterns to cut down on the amount necessary for repair work on these cars. Full implementation of the policy was in place by the 1870s when it was extended to cover locomotives as well as freight and passenger cars.

The Altoona shops produced some the country's first mail cars in 1886 with a small slot at the bottom of the mail car door for letters to be placed when a train stopped at the station.

In 1875, the Pennsylvania Railroad began testing new air brakes developed and patented by George Westinghouse. These brakes tested successfully, and the Pennsylvania Railroad became the first railroad to adopt them for all their cars in 1878.

In 1876, the Pennsylvania Railroad was the first railroad to introduce a 'limited' passenger train which made a limited number of stops on a Jersey City to Chicago train. In June 1887, the *Pennsylvania Limited* became the first regularly scheduled Pennsylvania Railroad train to be illuminated with electric lights.

On November 27, 1910, the Pennsylvania Railroad began passenger service into its new Pennsylvania Station in New York. In 1936, the railroad introduced passenger car air conditioning and sponge rubber cushions for seats to enhance passenger comfort.

In its early years, the Baldwin Locomotive Works built most of its locomotives, but by 1866 the railroad began building its own locomotives at its Altoona Works. The Consolidation (2-8-0 wheel arrangement) was the railroad's most popular type. Two are preserved at the Railroad Museum of Pennsylvania No. 1187 class H3 built by Altoona in 1888 and No. 2846 class H6sb built by Baldwin in 1905. The K4 Pacific (4-6-2 wheel arrangement) prototype No. 1737 delivered May 1914 proved to be successful delivering 44,460 pounds of tractive effort, which is the force that a locomotive can apply to its coupler to pull a train. It became the railroad's standard passenger locomotive.

In 1909, the Juniata Shops built No. 3998 DD1 prototype an electric locomotive that delivered 80,000 pounds of tractive effort and could reach 85 mph. A second prototype No. 3999 was built. With some adjustments made thirty-one additional units were built by Juniata Shops. They soon handled 600 trains daily at Pennsylvania Station. A few of these lasted until the 1960s. The first GG1 No. 4899 was rated at 4,620 horsepower and geared for 100 mph. It was renumbered No. 4800 and fifty-seven similar locomotives were built. Raymond Loewy was hired to refine the streamlined car body. He did not do the overall design. He suggested an all welded body and came up with the five gold pin stripes. The first production GG1

No. 4840 arrived August 1935. By 1943, there were 139 GG1 locomotives. Most survived the 1968 Penn Central merger. The last run of a GG1 was an excursion on October 29, 1983. The Pennsylvania Railroad's last new electric locomotives were 66 type E44 built by General Electric Company between 1960 and 1963. They were geared at 70 mph for freight service.

The Pennsylvania Railroad acquired its first diesel locomotive from the Electro Motive Division of General Motors Corporation in 1937. By 1947, dieselization began with units purchased from six different locomotive manufacturers. The railroad had to maintain six different sets of parts supply because the traction motors, engine blocks, and wheels were different. By 1957, steam locomotives were removed from active service.

The Pennsylvania Railroad had a dense network of passenger service. Improved highways, mass-produced automobiles, and airplanes had people switch from trains to cars. With new interstate highways, trucks could now provide faster service to many cities than the railroad, and the railroad faced traffic losses. During The Second World War, the Pennsylvania Railroad handled amazing volumes of freight and passenger traffic.

The 1957 recession drastically reduced revenues. The New York Central Railroad was in the same situation. With approval from the Interstate Commerce Commission on April 27, 1966, the Pennsylvania Railroad and New York Central Railroad merged on February 1, 1968 becoming the Penn Central Transportation Company. While the merger was to cut costs, it increased costs. Shipments were lost resulting in more trucks taking over Penn Central Transportation Company's dissatisfied customers. In addition to harsh weather and inflation, railroads had to compete with transportation modes that were subsidized. In 1968, Penn Central lost $400,000 per day. Bankruptcy was declared on June 1, 1970 with the railroad losing $800,000 per day. On April 1, 1976, Penn Central along with the Reading, Lehigh Valley, Central Railroad of New Jersey, Erie Lackawanna, and several smaller railroads were merged into Consolidated Rail Corporation (Conrail) which abandoned many lines, and by the mid 1980s started showing a profit. It was bought with Norfolk Southern Railway receiving about 58 percent and CSX Transportation receiving about 42 percent of Conrail's routes. Conrail ended independent operations on May 31, 1999.

CHAPTER 1

FREIGHT SERVICE

Freight service began twice a week on the Pennsylvania Railroad line from Harrisburg to Lewistown with 75 freight cars ordered in 1848. The number of freight cars peaked at 282,729 in 1919. However, freight car capacity increased from a total capacity of 13,648,772 tons in 1916 to 14,745,249 tons in 1931. There was a changeover from wood to steel cars that primarily took place between 1900 and 1925 with average car capacity increasing from 30.7 tons to 54.2 tons during that period. Increased use of higher capacity steel cars meant fewer cars were needed to carry the same tonnage. The Pennsylvania Railroad retired its last wooden flat car in 1934. In December 1916, the Pennsylvania Railroad's Juniata Shops completed a Decapod type steam locomotive with a 2-10-0 wheel arrangement. Following successful road tests, Juniata Shops built an additional 123 Decapods. Baldwin Locomotive Works received an order to build 475 Decapods in 1922, which was the largest order ever placed for a single type of steam locomotive. With a total of 598 Decapods, the Pennsylvania Railroad had the largest fleet of these locomotives that by 1924 were considered the standard heavy freight hauler of the railroad. In the 1930s, iron, steel, coal, and other raw materials provided a significant portion of the freight handled by the railroad. In addition, the railroad carried manufactured items, fresh fruits, vegetables, general produce, packing-house products, and lumber.

Serving the eastern seaports of New York, Philadelphia, Baltimore, and Norfolk, the railroad handled a large portion of the nation's import and export trade. During 1937, several freight lines were electrified including the Trenton Cutoff, the line along the east bank of the Susquehanna River to Perryville, Maryland, and from Rahway to South Amboy and Monmouth Junction. When the Second World War began in Europe in 1939, the Pennsylvania Railroad, recognizing the need for transporting materials for the Allies ordered 2,500 new freight cars, 20 electric locomotives, and 50,000 tons of rail. In addition it began repairs on 17,500 gondola and box cars that had been set aside for retirement.

Enola yard (across the Susquehanna River from Harrisburg, Pennsylvania) with repair shops, engine terminal and classification yards handled about 10,000 freight cars and about 200 trains daily in the 1950s. About 130 miles west of Enola was Altoona yard which had a large portion of its yard devoted to store freight cars that were scheduled for maintenance, rebuild, or repair at the Altoona shops. The largest railroad shops in the world were at Altoona with a workforce of 12,000. Conway yard twenty-three miles west of Pittsburgh was built to facilitate traffic flow at Pittsburgh. Meadows yard west of South Kearny, New Jersey was an origin/destination point for traffic destined for New Jersey. Morrisville, Pennsylvania yard mainly served United States Steel. West Philadelphia yard handled merchandise traffic plus coal from the lines that served anthracite mines. South Philadelphia yard handled coal and ore traffic. Northumberland yard (near Sunbury) handled cars for the Erie and Buffalo lines.

Soon after the Second World War began, the Pennsylvania Railroad borrowed a Chesapeake and Ohio class T1 Texas type steam locomotive and prepared drawings from it. The Altoona shops built 125 Texas type locomotives with a 2-10-4 wheel arrangement, and these locomotives handled freight on the railroad west of Altoona.

On December 31, 1945, the Pennsylvania Railroad operated 10,690 miles of railroad or 4.68 percent of the U.S. total of 228,473 miles but it handled 9.38 percent of the U.S. freight traffic and 16.69 percent of U.S. passenger traffic. It had 4,848 locomotives (11.26 percent of U.S.), 240,293 freight cars (13.59 percent of U.S. total, and 7,299 passenger cars (18.52 percent of U.S.) of the totals owned by Class I railroads which handled over 99 percent of the U.S. rail traffic. The railroad's freight cars assembled on a single track would extend 1,956 miles and fully loaded would carry over 13,000,000 tons. The railroad had a consistent policy of improving its motive power.

From 1900 to 1945, the Railroad retired over 10,000 obsolete locomotives. Decline of mineral traffic after The Second World War and the new Interstate Highway system resulted in a decline in freight revenues.

During 1952, the railroad began piggyback service whereby truck trailers are transported on flatcars. This was not a new idea as it was first introduced on the Chicago North Shore and Milwaukee Railroad in 1926.

Left: A Pennsylvania Railroad freight train is heading across the seven-arch Stone Bridge over the Conemaugh River in the city of Johnstown in Cambria County, Pennsylvania in this postcard dated January 16, 1917. The bridge was completed by the Pennsylvania Railroad during 1888. It is now used by the Norfolk Southern Railway.

Below: A westbound Pennsylvania Railroad train is coming out the west portal of the Gallitzin Tunnel in this postcard scene dated November 21, 1911. In contrast with the barren slope, the area between the tracks was covered with grass and shrubs. The Gallitzin Tunnel was later abandoned. On the right is the Allegheny Tunnel which was enlarged to accommodate two tracks with the first train going through the revamped tunnel on September 7, 1995.

Right: Pennsylvania Railroad class B6sb switcher with a 0-6-0 wheel arrangement No. 1687 is shown with the crew around 1917. This locomotive was built by the Pennsylvania Railroad at its Juniata Shops in February 1916.

Below: The borough of Huntingdon, Pennsylvania (approximately 32 miles east of Altoona and 98 miles west of Harrisburg, Pennsylvania) is the scene for Pennsylvania Railroad class K4s Pacific type steam locomotive No. 1436 with a 4-6-2 wheel arrangement passing by on October 7, 1946. The locomotive was built at the Pennsylvania Railroad's Juniata Shops on March 1918 and was scrapped on May 1948. (*Photograph by Bill Price, Robert Feddersen Collection*)

Above: On October 7, 1946, Pennsylvania Railroad class M1a Mountain type steam locomotive No. 6789 with a 4-8-2 wheel arrangement is passing through Huntingdon, Pennsylvania. This locomotive was built in April 1930 by Lima Locomotive Works as part of an order of 25 locomotives numbered 6775 to 6799. It was retired in January 1954. (*Photograph by Bill Price, Robert Feddersen Collection*)

Left: Under the signal bridge at Huntingdon, Pennsylvania, class M1a Mountain type steam locomotive No. 6743 is powering a Pennsylvania Railroad freight train on October 7, 1946. This locomotive was built in July 1930 by Baldwin Locomotive Works as part of an order of 50 locomotives numbered 6700 to 6749. The locomotive was sold for scrap in February 1956. (*Photograph by Bill Price, Robert Feddersen Collection*)

Above: Pennsylvania Railroad class M1a Mountain type locomotive No. 6752 is heading a freight train through Huntingdon, Pennsylvania on October 7, 1946. This locomotive was built in May 1930 as part of an order of 25 locomotives numbered 6750 to 6774 built at the Pennsylvania Railroad's Juniata Shops in Altoona. The locomotive was retired during 1952. (*Photograph by Bill Price, Robert Feddersen Collection*)

Right: In this October 7, 1946 scene, Pennsylvania Railroad class M1 Mountain type steam locomotive No. 6944 is at Huntingdon, Pennsylvania. This locomotive was built in November 1926 as part of an order of 175 locomotives numbered 6800 to 6974 built by the Baldwin Locomotive Works. The locomotive was scrapped in May 1949. (*Photograph by Bill Price, Robert Feddersen Collection*)

Above: Pennsylvania Railroad class M1 Mountain type steam locomotive No. 6898 is at Huntingdon, Pennsylvania on October 7, 1946. The locomotive was built by Baldwin locomotive Works in October 1926 and was retired in December 1955. (*Photograph by Bill Price, Robert Feddersen Collection*)

Below: On a sunny October 7, 1946, Pennsylvania Railroad class M1 Mountain type steam locomotive No. 6942 is passing through Huntingdon, PA. Built by Baldwin Locomotive Works in November 1926, the locomotive was sold for scrap in August 1956. (*Photograph by Bill Price, Robert Feddersen Collection*)

Right: There are two engineers, one conductor, and on the far right brakeman William C. Mowris in this June 16, 1949 view taken at Ash Street in Erie, Pennsylvania with 44-ton class GS4 diesel No. 9324, the first diesel locomotive in Pennsylvania Railroad yard service at Erie. The 400 horsepower locomotive was built by General Electric Company in 1949. (*Photograph by S. J. Modzelewski, William C. Mowris Collection*)

Below: Erie Dock Company (once a subsidiary of the Pennsylvania Railroad) car No. 7 is on display in this June 25, 2013 scene at the Lake Shore Railway Historical Society Museum located at the former Lake Shore and Michigan Southern Railway station at North East, Pennsylvania. Built around 1910 reportedly by the Atlas Car Company of Cleveland, Ohio, the electric (third rail) ore/coal car shunt according to the museum's data sheet, 'Operated on the Erie, PA, ore/coal docks until the mid 1950s; then at Whiskey Island, Cleveland until 1992'.

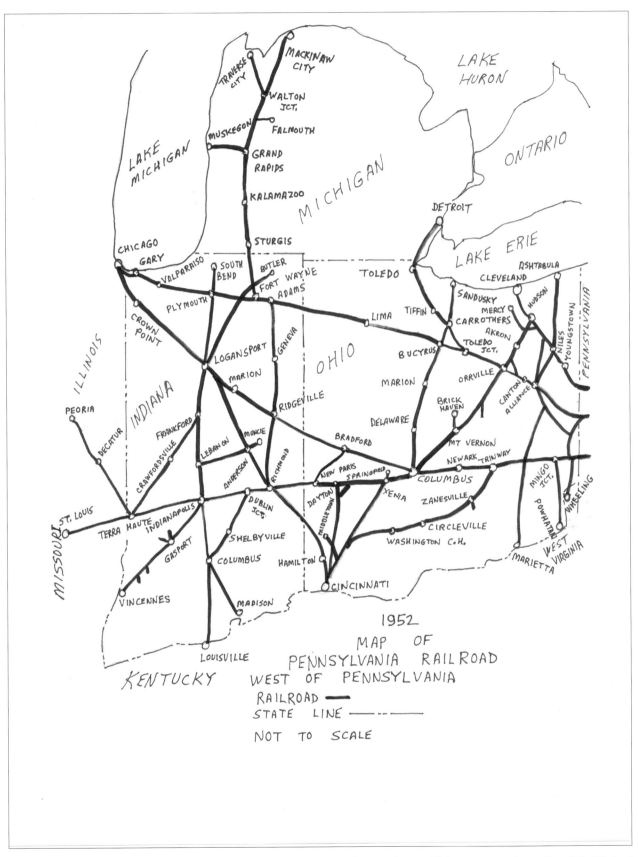

This 1952 map of the Pennsylvania Railroad shows the lines west of Pennsylvania. This was a massive railroad that linked the coalfields to the steel mills. It served the principal ports and carried more passengers than any other railroad in the United States. On June 30, 1910, the Pennsylvania Railroad operated 11,129 miles of track which declined by 4.5 percent to 10,690 miles of track on December 31, 1945 due to elimination of unprofitable lines.

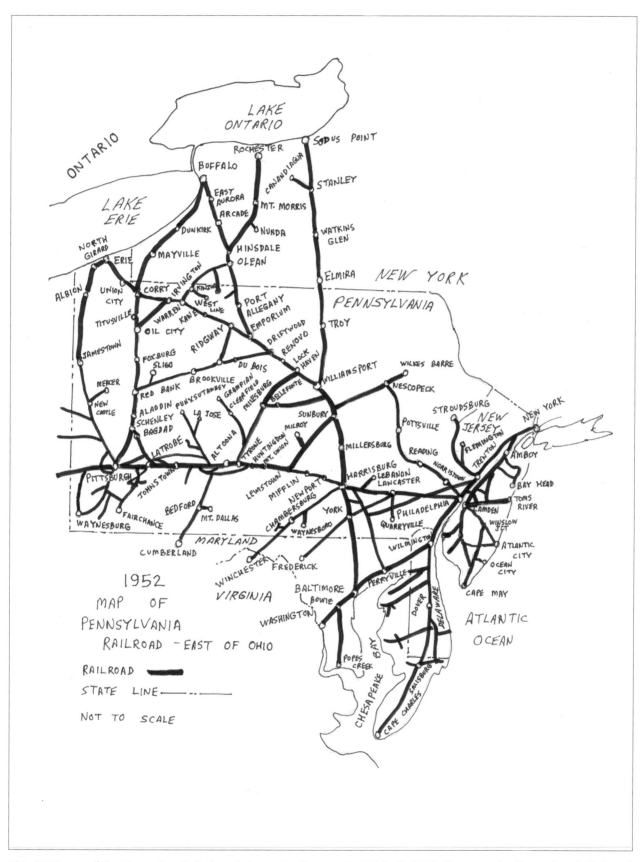

This 1952 map of the Pennsylvania Railroad shows the lines east of Ohio. In 1940, the states the Pennsylvania Railroad operated in (Pennsylvania, New York, New Jersey, Delaware, Maryland, West Virginia, Ohio, Indiana, Illinois, Michigan, Virginia, Kentucky, Missouri, and Washington, D.C.) had a population of 64,988,336 which was more than half the population of the continental United States of 131,669,275.

Above: Altoona, Pennsylvania is a busy place for the Pennsylvania Railroad in this June 9, 1948 scene. The Pennsylvania Railroad shops opened in Altoona in 1852, and additional buildings were added. By 1945, the Altoona shops of the Pennsylvania Railroad were the largest in the world. Portions of the Altoona shop facilities are now used by the Norfolk Southern Railway. (*Photograph by Edwin Wilde*)

Below: Under a clear sky, Pennsylvania Railroad class M1 Mountain type steam locomotive No. 6832 is at the borough of Newport in Perry County, Pennsylvania on May 30, 1952. This locomotive was built by Baldwin Locomotive Works in September 1926 and was retired in January 1954. (*Photograph by Bill Price, Robert Feddersen Collection*)

Above: Newport, Pennsylvania is the location for Pennsylvania Railroad class M1 Mountain type steam locomotive No. 6871 powering a freight train on May 30, 1952. The locomotive was built by Baldwin Locomotive Works in October 1926 and was scrapped in May 1950. (*Photograph by Bill Price, Robert Feddersen Collection*)

Below: Around 1950, Pennsylvania Railroad class I1s Decapod type steam locomotive with a 2-10-0 wheel arrangement No. 4458 is at work in Columbus Ohio. This locomotive was built in May 1923 by Baldwin Locomotive Works as part of an order of 100 locomotives numbered 4400 to 4499. In June 1942, the locomotive was converted to class I1sa and was retired in February 1952. (*Photograph by Robert Feddersen*)

Left: Pennsylvania Railroad class H6a Consolidation type steam locomotive with a 2-8-0 wheel arrangement No. 8084 is at the 59th Street railroad yard in Chicago around 1950. (*Photograph by Robert Feddersen*)

Below: At the 59th Street railroad yard in Chicago, Pennsylvania Railroad class H10s Consolidation type steam locomotive with a 2-8-0 wheel arrangement No. 8024 is ready for the next assignment. This locomotive was built by Baldwin Locomotive Works in December 1913 and was retired in April 1956. (*Photograph by Robert Feddersen*)

Above: In March 1954, Pennsylvania Railroad class K4s Pacific type steam locomotive with a 4-6-2 wheel arrangement No. 3752 is at the borough of Red Bank in Monmouth County, New Jersey. This locomotive was built in April 1920 at the Juniata Shops of the Pennsylvania Railroad at Altoona as part of a group of fifty locomotives numbered 3726 to 3775. The locomotive was retired in April 1958. (*Photograph by R. R. Wallin, Robert Feddersen Collection*)

Below: On the historic Rockville Bridge, Pennsylvania Railroad class M1a Mountain type steam locomotive No. 6779 is westbound on October 28, 1954. This locomotive was built by Lima Locomotive Works in March 1930 as part of an order of twenty-five locomotives numbered 6775 to 6799. It was sold for scrap in September 1959. (*Photograph by Bill Price, Robert Feddersen Collection*)

Above: On October 28, 1954, Pennsylvania Railroad class M1a Mountain type steam locomotive No. 6724 is heading a freight train at the west end of the Rockville Bridge. This locomotive was built by Baldwin Locomotive Works in May 1930 as part of an order of fifty locomotives numbered 6700 to 6749. It was modified to class M1b in February 1949 and was sold for scrap in September 1959. (*Photograph by Bill Price, Robert Feddersen Collection*)

Left: Pennsylvania Railroad class L1s Mikado type steam locomotive with a 2-8-2 wheel arrangement No. 3639 is powering a freight train at the west end of the Rockville Bridge on October 28, 1954. This locomotive was built by Baldwin Locomotive Works in April 1916 and was retired in May 1956. The Rockville Bridge crosses the Susquehanna River about five miles north of Harrisburg, Pennsylvania. (*Photograph by Bill Price, Robert Feddersen Collection*)

Right: In 1956 at Columbus, Ohio, Pennsylvania Railroad class J1 Texas type steam locomotive with a 2-10-4 wheel arrangement No. 6417 is getting ready for the next run. This locomotive was built in July 1943 at the Juniata Shops of the Pennsylvania Railroad. (*Photograph by Robert Feddersen*)

Below: Pennsylvania Railroad class L1s Mikado type steam locomotive No. 1638 is at the borough of Marysville in Perry County, Pennsylvania on January 20, 1957. This locomotive was built in March 1917 at the Juniata Shops of the Pennsylvania Railroad. It was sold for scrap in November 11, 1958. (*Photograph by R. R. Wallin, Robert Feddersen Collection*)

Above: On August 24, 1957, Pennsylvania Railroad class J1 Texas type steam locomotive No. 6404 is getting ready for departure at the city of Logansport in Cass County, Indiana. This locomotive was built by the Juniata Shops of the Pennsylvania Railroad in June 1943. (*Photograph by Darwin F. Simonaitis*)

Below: Near the unincorporated town of Anoka in Washington Township, Cass County, Indiana finds Pennsylvania Railroad class J1 Texas type steam locomotive No. 6152 powering an eastbound freight train heading for Columbus, Ohio on August 24, 1957. This locomotive was built in December 1943 by the Juniata Shops of the Pennsylvania Railroad. (*Photograph by Darwin F. Simonaitis*)

Above: Pennsylvania Reading Seashore Lines class E6s Atlantic type steam locomotive with a 4-4-2 wheel arrangement No. 1238 is at 4ᵗʰ Street in the city of Ocean City in Cape May County, New Jersey in 1950. This locomotive was built in May 1914 by the Pennsylvania Railroad's Juniata Shops and was retired in April 1951. (*Craig Knox Collection*)

Right: A group of Pennsylvania Railroad electric locomotives headed by class P5a locomotive No. 4743 are passing through the city of Coatesville in Chester County, Pennsylvania in 1962. This locomotive was built by Baldwin locomotive Works with Westinghouse Electric and Manufacturing Company motors in February 1935 and was scrapped in March 1962. The P5a was geared for ninety miles per hour for passenger service. In freight service, the P5a was geared for seventy miles per hour operation. (*Photograph by Craig Knox*)

Above: In 1962, Coatesville, Pennsylvania, about thirty-nine miles west of Philadelphia, Pennsylvania, is the scene for class P5a electric locomotive No. 4765 leading a train of locomotives. This locomotive was built by the General Electric Company in September 1932 and was scrapped in September 1961. (*Photograph by Craig Knox*)

Left: Pennsylvania Railroad class K4s Pacific type steam locomotive No. 7133 is ready for the next assignment around 1950. This locomotive was built at the Pennsylvania Railroad's Juniata Shops in July 1918 and was retired in September 1956.   (*Craig Knox Collection*)

Right: On March 31, 1964, a Pennsylvania Railroad type S12 diesel switcher, built by Baldwin Locomotive Works, is leaving the borough of West Chester in Chester County, Pennsylvania for a southbound run. This 1,200 horsepower locomotive had four type 362 Westinghouse motors and a type 480 Westinghouse generator. (*Photograph by Kenneth C. Springirth*)

Below: The local Pennsylvania Railroad freight train powered by a type S12 diesel switcher No. 8756, built by Baldwin Locomotive Works, is passing though Wawa, Pennsylvania on the railroad's West Chester Branch on March 31, 1964. (*Photograph by Kenneth C. Springirth*)

Above: Pennsylvania Railroad type RT-624 center cab diesel locomotives Nos. 8958 and 8965 are at Johnstown, Pennsylvania in November 1963. These 2,400 horsepower locomotives were built in 1951 by Baldwin Locomotive Works. (*Photograph by Regis F. Daly*)

Left: On September 11, 2011, former Pennsylvania Railroad diesel locomotive No. 9331 is preserved at the Strasburg Railroad in the borough of Strasburg in Lancaster County, Pennsylvania. This 44-ton locomotive was built by the General Electric Company in July 1948. (*Photograph by Kenneth C. Springirth*)

Above: At picturesque Horseshoe Curve finds Pennsylvania Railroad class K4s Pacific type locomotive No. 1361 on display on September 2, 1968. This locomotive was built by the Juniata Shops of the Pennsylvania Railroad in May 1918 and was retired in May 1956. During June 1957, the locomotive was placed on display at Horseshoe Curve and was replaced by type GP9 diesel locomotive No. 7048 in 1985. (*Photograph by Kenneth C. Springirth*)

Right: On April 14, 2012, Pennsylvania Railroad type GP9 diesel locomotive No. 7048 is on display at the Horseshoe Curve. This 1,750 horsepower locomotive was built in December 1955 by the Electro-Motive Division of General Motors Corporation (*Photograph by Kenneth C. Springirth*)

Above: With a light dusting of snow on the ground on December 27, 1970, Penn Central Transportation Company type GP40 diesel electric road switcher locomotive No. 3212, is leading a freight train through the city of Harrisburg in Dauphin County, Pennsylvania. This 4-axle 3,000 horsepower locomotive was built by the Electro-Motive Division of General Motors Corporation. (*Photograph by Kenneth C. Springirth*)

Left: On March 21, 1971, Penn Central Transportation Company 1,750 horsepower type GP9 diesel locomotive No. 7454, built by the Electro-Motive Division of General Motors Corporation, in the lineup of locomotives waits for the next assignment at the former Pennsylvania Railroad Wayne Street freight yard in Erie, Pennsylvania. (*Photograph by Kenneth C. Springirth*)

Above: At the former Pennsylvania Railroad Wayne Street yard in Erie, Pennsylvania in October 1973, are diesel locomotives No. 1761 (type F7A built for the New York Central Railroad in May 1952), No. 3460 (type F7B built in October 1952 as No. 2460 for the New York Central Railroad, and No. 1865 (type F7A built for the New York Central Railroad in October 1952). These locomotives, each rated 1,500 horsepower, were built by the Electro-Motive Division of General Motors Corporation. (*Photograph by Kenneth C. Springirth*)

Below: On October 1973, Penn Central Transportation Company 1,200 horsepower type SW7 diesel switcher No. 9097 is ready for service at the former Pennsylvania Railroad Wayne Street yard in Erie, Pennsylvania. This locomotive was originally built in January 1951 as No. 8871 for the Pennsylvania Railroad by the Electro-Motive Division of General Motors Corporation, (*Photograph by Kenneth C. Springirth*)

Left: The former Wayne Street Pennsylvania Railroad yard in Erie, Pennsylvania Railroad in June 1974 is the scene for Penn Central Transportation Company diesel locomotives No. 2420 (2,500 horsepower type C425 road switcher built by American Locomotive Company) and No. 9134 (1,200 horsepower type SW9 switcher built in March 1953 by the Electro-Motive Division of General Motors Corporation). (*Photograph by Kenneth C. Springirth*)

Below: Penn Central Transportation Company diesel locomotives No. 5689 (type GP7), No. 8968 (type SW9), and No. 5696 (type GP7) are on the turntable at the former Wayne Street yard of the Pennsylvania Railroad yard in Erie Pennsylvania in March 1975. Each of these locomotives was originally built for the New York Central Railroad by the Electro-Motive Division of General Motors Corporation. (*Photograph by Kenneth C. Springirth*)

Right: In April 1975, Penn Central Transportation Company type GP7 diesel locomotive No. 5752, built originally for the New York Central Railroad by the Electro-Motive Division of General Motors Corporation, is on the turntable at the former Wayne Street Pennsylvania Railroad yard in Erie, Pennsylvania. (*Photograph by Kenneth C. Springirth*)

Below: Basking in the sunshine of May 1975, Penn Central Transportation Company diesel locomotives 9064 (type SW7) and 9031 (type SW1200), each originally built for the Pennsylvania Railroad by the Electro-Motive Division of General Motors Corporation, are at the former Wayne Street Pennsylvania Railroad yard in Erie, Pennsylvania. (*Photograph by Kenneth C. Springirth*)

Left: In May 1975, Penn Central Transportation Company type GP7 diesel locomotive No. 5600, built by the Electro-Motive Division of General Motors Corporation, is on the turntable at the former Wayne Street Pennsylvania Railroad yard in Erie, Pennsylvania. (*Photograph by Kenneth C. Springirth*)

Below: At the former Wayne Street Pennsylvania Railroad yard in Erie, Pennsylvania, type GP7 Penn Central Transportation Company diesel locomotive No. 5700 (built originally for the New York Central Railroad by the Electro-Motive Division of General Motors Corporation) is ready for duty in May 1975. (*Photograph by Kenneth C. Springirth*)

Above: On October 22, 1978, Consolidated Rail Corporation diesel switchers No. 9177 (1,000 horsepower type NW2 built in July 1948 and later rebuilt) and No. 8846 (1,200 horsepower type SW7 built in February 1950) are at the former Wayne Street Pennsylvania Railroad yard in Erie, Pennsylvania. Both locomotives were built by the Electro-Motive Division of General Motors Corporation. (*Photograph by Kenneth C. Springirth*)

Right: Consolidated Rail Corporation 2,000 horsepower type GP38 diesel locomotive No. 7713 is powering a freight train crossing Norcross Road in Millcreek Township south of Erie, Pennsylvania on October 22, 1978. This locomotive was built originally for Penn Central Transportation Company in July 1969 by the Electro-Motive Division of General Motors Corporation.   (*Photograph by Kenneth C. Springirth*)

Above: A Consolidated Rail Corporation freight train from Erie to Warren, Pennsylvania (powered by 4,000 horsepower type GP40 diesel locomotives Nos. 3153 and 3149) is ready to cross Henderson Road in Millcreek Township south of Erie, Pennsylvania on March 14, 1982. Each locomotive was built in September 1968 for the Penn Central Transportation Company by the Electro-Motive Division of General Motors Corporation. (*Photograph by Kenneth C. Springirth*)

Left: In the snow covered undercut, the Erie to Warren local Consolidated Rail Corporation freight train (powered by type GP40 diesel locomotives Nos. 3153 and 3149) is about to pass under Lake Pleasant Road in Millcreek Township south of Erie, Pennsylvania on March 14, 1982. (*Photograph by Kenneth C. Springirth*)

Above: On March 28, 1982, Consolidated Rail Corporation local Erie to Warren freight train, headed by diesel locomotives No. 2192 (2,250 horsepower type GP30 built in August 1962 as No. 6119 for the New York Central Railroad) and No. 3124 (3,000 horsepower type GP40 built in August 1968 for Penn Central Transportation Company), is nearing the Henderson Road crossing in Millcreek Township south of Erie, Pennsylvania. Electro-Motive Division of General Motors Corporation built each locomotive. (*Photograph by Kenneth C. Springirth*)

Below: On a snowy January 1986, Allegheny Railroad 1,750 horsepower type CF7 diesel locomotives (still in a Santa Fe paint scheme) No. 2420 (rebuilt in February 1978) and No. 2521 (rebuilt in May 1974) are powering a freight train crossing Norcross Road in Millcreek Township south of Erie, Pennsylvania. These locomotives were originally 200 series F units built for the Santa Fe Railroad by the Electro-Motive Division of General Motors Corporation and were rebuilt at the Santa Fe shops in Cleburne, Texas. (*Photograph by Kenneth C. Springirth*)

Left: Allegheny Railroad type GP40 diesel locomotives No. 101 (originally Penn Central Transportation Company No. 3242) and No. 102 (originally Penn Central Transportation Company No. 3251) are crossing Pennsylvania Highway 426 west of the borough of Youngsville in Warren County, Pennsylvania powering a log train to Erie, Pennsylvania on March 25, 1986. Electro-Motive Division of General Motors Corporation built each locomotive in December 1968. (*Photograph by Michael B. Shannon*)

Below: An eastbound Allegheny Railroad freight train is crossing McClelland Avenue in Erie, Pennsylvania on June 9, 1990 headed by locomotives No. 106 (type GP35 built in June 1964 for the Union Pacific Railroad), No. 105 (type GP35 built in May 1964 for the Union Pacific Railroad), No. 101 (originally Penn Central Transportation Company No. 3242), and No. 102 (originally Penn Central Transportation Company No. 3251). Electro-Motive Division of General Motors Corporation built each locomotive. (*Photograph by Michel B. Shannon*)

CHAPTER 2

PASSENGER SERVICE

On September 1, 1849, the Pennsylvania Railroad began passenger service on the sixty-one-mile route from Harrisburg to Lewistown operating a daily one round trip. The passenger car roster was two passenger cars, one baggage car and two locomotives. Dining car service was inaugurated on the *Pennsylvania Limited* on May 6, 1882. In 1907, the all steel class P70 passenger coach was introduced by the Pennsylvania Railroad. During the peak year of 1923, the railroad had 8,301 passenger cars of which 68 percent were of steel construction. By 1932, there were only 99 wooden cars out of a total of 7,227 passenger cars.

The Depression resulted in a decline to 6,558 passenger cars by 1933, but the Second World War resulted in an increase to 7,299 by December 31, 1945. Construction of the Pennsylvania Station in New York (described as the largest and handsomest in the world) began in 1903 and was completed in 1910. It was in use for over fifty years. Electrification of Philadelphia area commuter lines with an 11,000 volt AC overhead catenary system was completed on the Paoli line on September 12, 1915; Chestnut Hill line on March 30, 1918; Wilmington line on September 30, 1928; Media/West Chester line on December 2, 1928; Trenton line on June 29, 1930; and Norristown line on July 20, 1930.

On December 15, 1933, the 30th Street Station in Philadelphia was opened serving passenger trains on the New York-Washington line along with suburban runs. In 1933, the New York–Washington trains featured air-conditioned cars. On February 10, 1935, electric train service from New York City reached Washington D.C. The first electrically powered passenger train arrived in Harrisburg on January 15, 1938. During the mid 1960s, experiments were conducted that led to the introduction of the Metroliner (100 mph multiple unit trains designed and built by the Budd Company). Technical problems prevented the Metroliners from entering service until 1969 a year after the Pennsylvania Railroad merged with the New York Central.

Serving the most heavily populated part of the United States, the Pennsylvania Railroad before the Depression carried 20 percent of rail passengers in the USA on its intercity, local, and commuter trains. In 1881, the Pennsylvania Railroad introduced the *Pennsylvania Limited* from Jersey City to Chicago. It featured a barber shop, dining car, sleeping cars, and an observation sleeper lounge. On June 15, 1902, the *Pennsylvania Special* began serving the 908-mile run from Chicago via Pittsburgh to New York run in 20 hours. It became the *Broadway Limited* on November 24, 1912. On June 15, 1938, the *Broadway Limited's* travel time from New York to Chicago was reduced to sixteen hours. The Amtrak timetable Winter Spring 2013 shows the *Pennsylvanian* leaves New York at 10:52 a.m. arriving at Pittsburgh at 8:05 p.m. where the connecting train leaves Pittsburgh at 11:59 p.m. arriving in Chicago at 8:45 a.m. (central time) requiring 22 hours and 53 minutes. The *Congressional Limited* began service on December 7, 1885 from New York to Washington D.C. It was upgraded in 1952 with stainless steel streamlined equipment built by the Budd Company of Philadelphia.

Second to the New York Washington Corridor in terms of ridership was the Pennsylvania Railroad from Philadelphia via Harrisburg to Pittsburgh. Principal New York to Pittsburgh trains included the *Pittsburgher, Duquesne, Juniata, Pittsburgh Night Express, New Yorker,* and *Iron City Express.* New York City to Chicago service featured the *Broadway Limited* and *General* which made the trip in sixteen hours plus *Manhattan Limited, Fort Dearborn, Progress Limited, New Yorker, Admiral, Gotham Limited,* and *Pennsylvania Limited.* The Third corridor was from New York via Pittsburgh, Columbus, and Indianapolis to St. Louis, which was served by the *Spirit of St. Louis* and the more basic *St. Louisan* with the *Jeffersonian* added in 1941 and *Penn Texas* in 1948.

Erie to Philadelphia service was provided by the *Northern Express* and *Southern Express.* The Pennsylvania Railroad operated extensive suburban commuter service in the New York and Philadelphia regions plus smaller operations in Pittsburgh, Chicago and Baltimore/ Washington.

WORLD'S FASTEST LOCOMOTIVE
Pennsylvania Railroad's No. 7002—Record 127.1 Miles an Hour

Chicago Railroad Fair 1949

Above: Pennsylvania Railroad class E2 Atlantic type steam locomotive No. 7002 is on display at the Chicago Railroad Fair of 1949 in this postcard view. The locomotive was actually No. 8063 that was altered to resemble No. 7002 that had been scrapped. This locomotive reportedly set a speed record handling the *Broadway Limited* on June 12, 1905 reaching 127.1 miles per hour between AY tower and Elida, Ohio.

Below: In this 1910 postcard scene, a Pennsylvania Railroad passenger train is leaving the station at Monongahela City in Washington County, Pennsylvania. There was frequent passenger service from Pittsburgh via Monongahela City to Brownsville during 1916.

Above: Pennsylvania Station on Liberty Avenue in downtown Pittsburgh, Pennsylvania was a busy place with much pedestrian traffic and a number of Pittsburgh Railways trolley cars in this postcard view. Constructed during 1898 to 1903, the 12-story station, once used by 40,000 passengers daily, was a center point on the Pennsylvania Railroad with lines radiating east and west.

Below: This postcard post marked July 24, 1931 advertises the *Broadway Limited*. The train was operated by the Pennsylvania Railroad daily between New York and Chicago. When Amtrak took over the nationwide passenger operation on May 1, 1971, the *Broadway Limited* was continued. On November 12, 1990, the train was rerouted to use the former Baltimore and Ohio Railroad west of Pittsburgh to Chicago and made its last run on September 9, 1995.

Horseshoe Curve, P. R. R., near Altoona, Pa.

Above: In this postcard scene postmarked March 6, 1916, a Pennsylvania Railroad passenger train is negotiating the Horseshoe Curve. Construction of the Horseshoe Curve began in 1850 with men using picks and shovels completing it for the opening day February 15, 1854.

Left: The *Gotham Limited* is traversing the Horseshoe Curve in this postcard scene. This Pennsylvania Railroad passenger train operated between New York City and Chicago. In the 1940s, over fifty daily passenger trains used the Horseshoe Curve along with many freight and military trains.

Above: A Pennsylvania Railroad passenger train is at the borough of Blairsville in Indiana County, Pennsylvania. This postcard is postmarked April 9, 1915. In 1916, there were a number of local passenger trains operating from Pittsburgh via Aspinwall, Tarentum, Freeport, Kiskiminetas Junction, Bagdad, to Blairsville.

Below: A Pennsylvania Railroad passenger train is at Coatesville, Pennsylvania in this postcard postmarked December 22, 1910. Numerous trains stopped at Coatesville in 1916 on the Philadelphia to Harrisburg line.

453

PENNSYLVANIA SYSTEM
PENNSYLVANIA RAILROAD
Adams Express Company

Table 80—CENTRAL DIVISION.—Williamsport and Renovo Divisions.

[Detailed timetable of train schedules with numerous train numbers (561, 8509, 575, 631, 501, 515, 571, 541, 579, 503, 35-577, and 580, 574, 630, 500, 578, 570, 560, 588, 576, 506, 562, 578) showing times for stations between New York/Philadelphia/Washington/Baltimore and Buffalo/Erie via Harrisburg, Sunbury, Williamsport, Renovo, Emporium, Ridgway, Kane, Warren, Corry, and Erie. Dated May 28, 1916.]

Table 81—RIDGWAY BRANCH.
May 28, 1916.

Table 32—JOHNSON-BURG R.R. BRANCH.
Train lvs. Johnsonburg †8 00 p.m. for Glen Hazel (6.2 mls.), Straight (10.4 mls.), Instanter (12.2 mls.), Smiths Run (14.9 mls.), Woodvale (18.4 mls.), arr. Clermont (20.2 mls.) †345 p.m. Lvs. Clermont †1040 a.m., arr. Johnsonburg 11 25 a.m.

THROUGH CAR ARRANGEMENT.—(Coaches on all trains unless otherwise noted.)

No. 501—Parlor Car and Restaurant Car Philadelphia to Harrisburg. Parlor Car Washington to Harrisburg. Restaurant Car Baltimore to Harrisburg.

No. 35-577—Drawing-room Sleeping Car Philadelphia to Buffalo (open 10 00 p.m.). Drawing-room Sleeping Car Washington to Buffalo.

No. 503—Sleeping Car Philadelphia to Williamsport (open at 10 00 p.m. and may be occupied until 7 30 a.m.). Drawing-room Sleeping Car Pittsburgh to Wilkes-Barre, except Saturdays (via Harrisburg and Sunbury). Drawing-room Sleeping Car New York to Williamsport, leaving New York 8 00 p.m. (may be occupied until 7 30 a.m.)

No. 579—Drawing-room Sleeping Car Philadelphia to Erie. Drawing-room Sleeping Car Washington to Oil City (on Northern Division train No. 952 from Corry). Cafe Coach Kane to Erie.

No. 541—Sleeping Car N. Y. to Harrisburg (open Penna. Sta. 10 00 p.m.).

No. 571—Parlor Car and Restaurant Car Washington to Buffalo. Parlor Car Philadelphia to Buffalo.

No. 575—Drawing-room Sleeping Cars Washington to Buffalo and Philadelphia to Buffalo. Broiler Buffet Parlor Car Philadelphia to Harrisburg.

No. 515—Broiler Buffet Parlor Car Philadelphia to Williamsport week-days. Parlor Car and Restaurant Car Washington to Harrisburg.

No. 631—Week-days—Parlor Car Philadelphia to Williamsport; Washington to Harrisburg. Restaurant Car Philadelphia to Harrisburg.

No. 631—Sundays—Sleeping Cars, Restaurant Car and Parlor Car New York to Harrisburg. Parlor Car Washington to Harrisburg.

No. 561—Drawing-room Sleeping Car Pittsburgh to Wilkes-Barre, leaving Pittsburgh Saturdays only (via Harrisburg and Sunbury). Sleeping Car New York to Harrisburg (open 10 00 p.m.).

No. 578—Broiler Buffet Parlor Car Williamsport to Philadelphia week-days. Drawing-room Parlor Car Harrisburg to Washington daily.

No. 500—Broiler Buffet Parlor Car Harrisburg to Philadelphia.

No. 570—Parlor Cars and Restaurant Car Buffalo to Washington. Parlor Cars Buffalo to Philadelphia. Restaurant Car Harrisburg to Phila.

No. 574—Drawing-room Sleeping Car Buffalo to Philadelphia. Drawing-room Sleeping Car Buffalo to Washington. Restaurant Car Harrisburg to Washington.

No. 580—Drawing-room Sleeping Car Erie to Phila. Drawing-room Sleeping Car Oil City to Washington on Northern Division train No. 953 from Oil City to Corry (running on No. 574 from Williamsport). Restaurant Car Harrisburg to Washington. Cafe Coach Erie to Kane.

No. 576—Drawing-room Sleeping Car Buffalo to Washington and Buffalo to Philadelphia (open 10 00 a.m.). Restaurant Car Harrisburg to Baltimore and Harrisburg to Philadelphia.

No. 506—Drawing-room Sleeping Car Williamsport to New York (open 9 00 p.m., may be occupied until 7 30 a.m.). Sleeping Car Williamsport to Philadelphia (open 9 00 p.m., may be occupied until 7 00 a.m. week-days; 8 00 a.m. Sundays).

No. 630—Parlor Car Williamsport to Phila.; Harrisburg to Washington.

No. 568—Sleeping Car (open 10 00 p.m.) Harrisburg to N.Y.; Wilkes-Barre to Pittsburgh (via Sunbury and Harrisburg) (Drawing-room).

The May 28, 1916 Pennsylvania Railroad timetable shows three trains daily in each direction between Philadelphia and Erie, Pennsylvania. In addition, there was a daily morning train leaving Kane at 6:55 a.m. arriving in Erie at 10:15 a.m. It left Erie at 1 p.m. and arrived in Kane, Pennsylvania at 4:20 p.m.

P. R. R. Curve and Rockville Bridge, longest Stone Bridge in the world, Harrisburg, Pa.

Above: In this postcard postmarked March 3, 1916, a Pennsylvania Railroad passenger train is eastbound on the 3,820-foot long Rockville Bridge north of Harrisburg, Pennsylvania. The 48-stone masonry arch Rockville Bridge was completed in April 1902 by the Pennsylvania Railroad.

Right: It is amazing to see the size of the J. C. Blair manufacturing facility at 6th and Penn Streets in Huntingdon, Pennsylvania (built in 1889) with a Pennsylvania Railroad passenger train passing the building in this postcard. J. C. Blair of Huntingdon County was the inventor of the paper tablet, and each tablet featured a graphically striking image that created in potential customers a desire to own the image even if they did not need a tablet.

449

PENNSYLVANIA SYSTEM
PENNSYLVANIA RAILROAD

Adams Express Company

NORTHERN DIVISION—Conemaugh and Allegheny Divisions—Continued.
Table 67—TRAINS BETWEEN PITTSBURGH AND KITTANNING.

May 28, 1916.

	Mls	933	6901	9001	6957	9011	6905	935	6805	9016	937	6907	6909	9017	6959	9019	6913	911	6915	6945	9027	6841	6961	6963	9021	6943
		AM	AM	AM	AM	AM	AM	Noon	PM	PM	PM	PM	PM	PM	PM	PM	PM	PM	PM	AM	Noon	PM	PM	PM	PM	PM

(Table continued — extensive station-by-station timetable listing stations from Pittsburgh and East Liberty through Nadine, Sandy Creek, Verona, Edgewater, Oakmont, Hulton, Black's Run, Barking, Logan's Ferry, Parnassus, New Kensington, Arnold, Valley Camp, Edgecliff, Braeburn, Metcalf, McKean, Garver's Ferry, Kiskiminetas Jn., Schenley, Aladdin, Godfrey, Johnetta, Kelly, Logansport, Rosston, Ford City, Manorville, to Kittanning.)

(Eastern time.)

	6916	6950	6918	6920	9002	9024	928	6922	926	9006	6924	9008	900	6926	9012	6928	924	6952	6932	6934	6936	6938	9022	6954	9004	6968

(Table continued — return direction timetable listing stations from Kittanning, Manorville, Ford City, Rosston, Logansport, Kelly, Johnetta, Godfrey, Aladdin, Schenley, Kiskiminetas Jn., Garver's Ferry, McKean, Metcalf, Braeburn, Edgecliff, Valley Camp, Arnold, New Kensington, Parnassus, Logan's Ferry, Barking, Black's Run, Hulton, Oakmont, Edgewater, Verona, Sandy Creek, Nadine, Brilliant, Butler Street, Fifty-fourth St., Forty-third St., Thirty-fourth St., East Liberty, to Pittsburgh.)

Table 68—REDSTONE BRANCH.—Monongahela Division.

7870	7866	7860	7864	7816	7814	7810	7804	7800	Mls	*May 28, 1916.*	7815	7819	7823	7829	7831	7875	7879	7881	7885

(Redstone Branch timetable listing Pittsburgh, Braznell, Tippecanoe, Smock, Upper Middletown, Vance Mill Jn., Bute, Vance Mill June., Redstone Junction, Uniontown.)

For additional express trains between Pittsburgh and Kittanning, see preceding page.

* Daily; † daily, except Sunday; § Sunday only; *a* stops on signal to leave passengers from Pittsburgh and East Liberty and to take for Buffalo; *k* stops Saturday only; *r* stops Sunday only; *x* stops May 28th to September 30th, inclusive. + Coupon stations; ‡ Leaving time only. + Coupon stations; ♦ Telegraph stations.

The Pennsylvania Railroad May 28, 1916 timetable between Pittsburgh and Kittanning shows numerous passenger trains with frequent service particularly between Pittsburgh and Braeburn. The section of the railroad from Kiskiminetas Junction via Aladdin to the Logansport Mine two miles south of Ford City is now operated by the Kiski Junction Railroad.

Right: In this postcard postmarked June 19, 1909, a Pennsylvania Railroad passenger train is at the Lewistown Junction, Pennsylvania station where a Lewistown and Reedsville Electric Railway Company trolley car is there providing service every twenty minutes from the station to Lewistown. Trolley car service from Lewistown via Burnham and Yeagertown to Reedsville was every thirty minutes. Trolley car service began from Lewistown to Burnham on March 13, 1900 and was extended to Reedsville in 1901. Trolley car service ended on July 1, 1932.

Below: Passengers are waiting for the next train at the Pennsylvania Railroad passenger station at the borough of Wilmerding in Allegheny County, Pennsylvania. This station, 13.7 miles from downtown Pittsburgh via rail, was served by numerous trains and was on the main line between Philadelphia and Pittsburgh.

Penna. R. R. Station, Lewistown Junction, Pa.

P. R. R. STATION, WILMERDING, PA.

490

PENNSYLVANIA SYSTEM

PENNSYLVANIA LINES WEST OF PITTSBURGH

Adams Express Co.

Pennsylvania Company

Official Local Time-Tables—May, 1916.

ERIE AND ASHTABULA DIVISION—ERIE & PITTSBURGH RAILROAD

Table 8—BETWEEN PITTSBURGH AND ERIE.

Mls.	(Central time.)	405	1719	415	445	333	455	955	475	343
....		A M	A M	A M	Noon	P M	P M	P M	P M	P M
0	Pittsburgh+ lve.	*6 25	*7 15	*8 20	†12 00	*1 30	*2 50	†4 30	*5 45	*7 05
1.0	Federal Street+	6 30	7 20	8 25	12 05	1 35	2 55	4 34	5 50	7 10
12.5	Sewickley	6 47	7 35	8 40	12 22	- -	3 10	4 53	- -	c -
25.7	Rochester+	7 09	7 56	8 58	12 40	2 04	3 28	5 13	6 19	7 40
28.4	New Brighton+	7 15	8 01	9 04	12 46	- -	3 34	5 21	- -	- -
29.2	Kenwood	- -	- -	- -	- -	- -	- -	5 25	- -	- -
30.2	Beaver Falls+	7 23	8 09	9 10	12 55	2 15	3 40	5 30	b -	7 50
34.8	Homewood	7 35	- -	- -	- -	- -	3 50	- -	- -	- -
36.2	Koppel	7 37	8 23	d -	1 07	- -	3 52	5 42	- -	- -
39.7	Crescentdale	7 41	8 27	d -	1 10	- -	3 55	- -	- -	- -
40.6	Wampum	7 45	- -	- -	1 13	- -	3 59	5 47	- -	- -
43.9	Moravia	7 51	- -	- -	- -	- -	- -	5 53	- -	- -
47.4	Mahoningtown	8 05	8 49	- -	1 27	2 47	4 12	6 03	- -	8 21
49.7	New Castle+	8 15	8 54	9 45	1 35	2 50	4 20	P M	7 05	8 25
60.0	Pulaski	8 30	A M	- -	1 52	P M	4 34	....	- -	P M
64.6	West Middlesex	8 39	....	- -	1 59	Via Low Grade.	4 44	....	- -	Via Low Grade.
67.4	Wheatland	8 44	....	- -	- -		4 51	....	- -	
68.5	Farrell	8 47	....	10 09	2 07		4 54	....	7 30	
69.8	Sharon+	8 55	....	10 15	2 15		5 05	....	7 35	
73.0	Sharpsville	9 03	....	10 23	2 23		5 13	....	7 43	
75.6	Clarksville	9 06	....	- -	2 26		5 18	....	- -	
78.7	Transfer	9 15	....	- -	2 31		5 25	....	- -	
82.8	Shenango	9 20	....	10 38	2 37		5 31	....	7 55	
84.4	Greenville+	9 28	....	10 51	2 50		5 45	....	8 01	
90.5	Jamestown+	9 40	....	11 02	3 05	....	5 58	....	8 12	....
96.2	Westford	9 50	....	- -	3 16	....	6 08	....	- -	....
99.6	Espyville	9 55	....	- -	3 22	....	6 13	....	- -	....
103.6	Linesville	10 10	....	11 25	3 30	....	6 20	....	8 35	....
107.7	Summit	A M	....	11 30	3 35	....	P M	....	s -	....
111.2	Conneautville	....	....	11 36	3 45	....	....	....	s -	....
114.0	Springboro	....	....	11 41	3 50	....	....	....	s -	....
120.3	Albion	....	....	11 48	4 02	....	....	....	s -	....
130.7	North Girard	....	....	- -	- -	....	....	....	- -	....
146.0	Erie+ arr.	....	....	12 30	4 50	....	....	....	9 45	....
....		....	....	Noon	P M	....	....	....	P M	....

(Central time.)	404	914	414	302	424	332	454	474	374	1340
	....	....	A M	....	A M	....	....	P M	....	....
Erie lve.	....	....	†5 50	....	*9 15	....	....	*4 00	....	....
North Girard	....	....	- -	....	- -	....	....	- -	....	....
Albion	....	....	6 31	....	s -	....	....	4 38	....	....
Springboro	....	....	6 40	....	s -	....	....	4 45	....	....
Conneautville	....	....	6 48	....	s -	....	....	4 54	....	....
Summit	A M	....	6 55	....	s -	....	P M	5 02	....	....
Linesville	*5 10	....	7 05	....	10 22	....	*1 55	5 12	....	....
Espyville	5 15	....	- -	....	- -	....	2 02	5 17	....	....
Westford	5 22	....	- -	....	- -	....	2 12	- -	....	....
Jamestown	5 35	....	7 25	....	10 41	....	2 22	5 33	....	....
Greenville	5 45	....	7 35	Via Low Grade.	10 51	Via Low Grade.	2 32	5 45	....	Via Low Grade.
Shenango	5 50	....	7 40		10 57		2 37	5 52	....	
Transfer	5 57	....	7 47		- -		2 45	- -	....	
Clarksville	6 01	....	7 50		- -		2 50	- -	....	
Sharpsville	6 05	....	7 55		11 11		2 55	6 06	....	
Sharon	6 13	....	8 07		11 22		3 10	6 15	....	
Farrell	6 15	....	8 09		11 24		3 13	6 18	....	
Wheatland	- -	....	8 14		- -		- -	- -	....	
West Middlesex	6 23	....	8 19		s -		3 21	- -	....	
Pulaski	6 29	....	8 26	A M	s -	P M	3 32	- -	P M	P M
New Castle	6 55	A M	8 50	*9 20	11 55	*3 48	4 00	6 50	*7 00	*7 58
Mahoningtown	7 00	†8 25	- -	9 25	- -	3 53	4 08	6 55	7 05	8 03
Moravia	- -	8 32	- -	- -	- -	- -	- -	- -	7 19	- -
Wampum	7 10	8 40	- -	- -	- -	n4 11	4 20	- -	- -	- -
Crescentdale	7 12	8 42	- -	- -	12 12	- -	4 22	- -	- -	- -
Koppel	7 19	8 52	- -	- -	12 18	- -	4 30	- -	7 40	- -
Homewood	- -	- -	- -	- -	- -	- -	4 40	- -	- -	- -
Beaver Falls	7 31	9 08	9 22	10 00	12 34	4 27	4 47	7 27	7 57	8 42
Kenwood	- -	- -	- -	- -	- -	- -	- -	- -	- -	- -
New Brighton	7 36	9 15	9 30	- -	12 38	- -	4 52	7 32	8 02	- -
Rochester	7 42	9 22	9 36	10 11	12 44	4 37	4 58	7 38	8 08	- -
Sewickley	8 00	9 44	9 55	- -	1 03	- -	5 28	7 56	8 39	9 14
Federal Street arr.	8 20	10 05	10 15	10 45	1 20	5 10	5 50	8 15	9 10	9 35
Pittsburgh arr.	8 25	10 10	10 20	10 50	1 25	5 15	5 55	8 20	9 15	9 40
	A M	A M	A M	A M	P M	P M	P M	P M	P M	P M

Table 9—BETWEEN NEW CASTLE AND CLEVELAND—VIA YOUNGSTOWN.

Ms.	(Central time.)	7050	3190	7450	3330	7150	1340
....		A M	A M	A M	P M	P M	P M
0	New Castle lve.	*7 00	*8 30	*11 30	*2 25	*7 10	*7 58
2.3	Mahoningtown	7 05	8 35	11 35	2 30	7 15	8 03
3.4	Lawrence Junction	- -	8 42	- -	2 42	- -	8 17
8.4	Edenburg	7 12	g -	11 42	- -	- -	- -
11.3	Hillsville	7 15	g -	11 46	- -	- -	- -
14.1	Lowellville	7 20	g -	11 51	- -	- -	- -
16.7	Struthers	7 26	g -	11 55	- -	y -	- -
22.2	Youngstown	7 45	9 20	12 15	3 15	7 50	8 50
27.1	Girard	7 54	9 30	12 24	- -	y -	- -
31.6	Niles	8 05	9 47	12 35	3 38	8 10	9 12
42.8	Newton Falls	A M	A M	Noon	3 54	P M	9 29
57.7	Ravenna	....	....	....	4 14	....	9 50
69.6	Hudson	....	....	....	4 30	....	10 05
75.7	Macedonia	....	....	....	- -	....	- -
81.1	Bedford	....	....	....	- -	....	- -
87.6	Harvard Avenue	....	....	....	4 55	....	m -
90.4	Woodland Avenue	....	....	....	5 01	....	- -
91.8	Euclid Avenue	....	....	....	5 08	....	10 43
95.0	Cleveland arr.	....	....	....	5 20	....	10 55
....		....	....	....	P M	....	P M

Ms.	(Central time.)	1724	302	744	332	374	1340	704
....		....	A M	....	P M	....	P M	....
0	Cleveland lve.	....	*7 00	....	*1 30	....	*5 30	....
3.2	Euclid Avenue	....	7 11	....	1 40	....	5 40	....
4.6	Woodland Avenue	....	x -	....	x -	....	- -	....
7.4	Harvard Avenue	....	x -	....	x -	....	- -	....
13.9	Bedford	....	- -	....	- -	....	- -	....
19.3	Macedonia	....	- -	....	- -	....	- -	....
25.4	Hudson	....	7 45	....	2 17	....	6 20	....
37.3	Ravenna	....	8 02	....	2 33	....	- -	....
52.2	Newton Falls	A M	8 22	P M	2 53	P M	- -	P M
63.4	Niles	*6 52	8 40	*2 41	3 11	*6 10	7 16	*10 45
67.9	Girard	7 03	- -	2 51	- -	6 19	- -	10 54
72.8	Youngstown	7 15	9 05	3 05	3 33	6 40	7 35	11 05
78.3	Struthers	7 25	- -	3 17	- -	- -	- -	11 16
80.9	Lowellville	7 28	- -	3 22	- -	- -	- -	11 19
83.7	Hillsville	- -	- -	3 27	- -	- -	- -	- -
86.6	Edenburg	- -	- -	3 34	- -	- -	- -	- -
91.6	Lawrence Junction	- -	9 38	- -	4 02	7 15	8 18	- -
92.5	Mahoningtown	7 50	9 45	3 45	4 05	7 18	8 21	11 40
95.0	New Castle arr.	7 55	9 50	3 50	4 10	7 23	8 25	11 45
....		A M	A M	P M	P M	P M	P M	P M

Table 10—BETWEEN PITTSBURGH AND OIL CITY.

Ms.	(Central time.)	No. 905	No. 945	No. 955
....	Pittsburgh+ lve.	*6 25 A M	†12 00 Noon	†4 30 P M
....	Mahoningtown	8 10 »	1 35 P M	6 03 »
0	New Castle+	8 30 »	1 50 »	6 20 »
7.8	Wilmington Junc+	8 48 »	2 07 »	- -
9.0	Neshannock Falls	8 51 »	2 09 »	6 41 »
12.3	Volant	8 58 »	2 13 »	6 45 »
14.7	Leesburg	9 05 »	2 23 »	6 55 »
16.8	Millburn	9 10 »	2 25 »	6 57 »
18.6	Hope Mills	9 13 »	2 29 »	7 01 »
21.5	Mercer+	9 20 »	2 40 »	7 15 »
22.4	Houston Junction	9 23 »	2 42 »	7 18 »
26.6	Jackson Centre+	9 31 »	2 50 »	7 24 »
32.7	Coulson	9 40 »	3 05 »	7 38 »
35.1	Stoneboro+ arr.	*9 55 »	3 25 P M	†7 45 »
	Stoneboro+ lve.	†9 55 »	....	*7 48 »
36.4	Sandy Lake	9 58 »	....	7 51 »
46.8	Polk	10 15 »	....	8 09 »
55.7	Franklin	10 30 »	....	8 30 »
65.8	Oil City, West Side lv.	10 50 »	....	*8 55 P M
	Oil City, East Side ar.	†11 05 A M	....	....

Mls.	(Central time.)	No. 914	No. 944	No. 974
0	Oil City, East Side lv.	....	†1 15 P M	....
	Oil City, West Side	*5 45 A M	1 20 »	....
9.2	Franklin	6 05 »	1 37 »	....
18.1	Polk	6 20 »	1 51 »	....
28.4	Sandy Lake	6 39 »	2 07 »	....
30.7	Stoneboro arr.	*6 42 »	2 10 »	....
	Stoneboro lve.	†6 50 »	2 10 »	*5 05 P M
33.1	Coulson	6 53 »	- -	5 08 »
39.2	Jackson Centre	7 11 »	2 28 »	5 21 »
43.4	Houston Junction	7 19 »	2 35 »	5 30 »
44.3	Mercer	7 25 »	2 40 »	5 32 »
47.2	Hope Mills	7 28 »	- -	5 33 »
49.0	Millburn	7 33 »	- -	5 38 »
51.1	Leesburg	7 38 »	2 55 »	5 45 »
53.5	Volant	7 45 »	3 00 »	5 50 »
56.8	Neshannock Falls	7 50 »	3 07 »	5 57 »
58.0	Wilmington Junc	7 55 »	3 12 »	6 03 »
65.8	New Castle arr.	8 15 »	3 35 »	6 35 »
68.3	Mahoningtown	8 25 »	3 45 »	6 45 »
115.5	Pittsburgh arr.	†10 10 A M	5 15 P M	*8 20 P M

EXPLANATION OF SIGNS.

* Daily; † daily, except Sunday; *b* stops to take passengers for the E. & A. Division; *c* stops to take passengers for Cleveland and E. & A. Division points or Lawrence Junction; *d* stops to leave passengers from Pittsburgh and Sewickley; *g* stops to leave from east of Homewood; *m* stops to leave passengers; *n* stops to take for Pittsburgh or points beyond; *s* stops Sunday only; *x* stops on signal for passengers for Newton Falls or beyond; *y* stops for passengers to or from Niles and stations west.

+ Coupon stations.

♁ Telegraph stations

For Through Time-Tables and Through Car Service, see pages 472-478.

The May 1916 Pennsylvania Railroad timetable Table 8 shows three trains in each direction Monday through Saturday between Erie and Pittsburgh with two in each direction on Sunday. There was additional service between Linesville and Pittsburgh making it possible to commute to Pittsburgh by train. Table 9 shows service between New Castle, Pennsylvania and Cleveland, Ohio via Youngstown, Ohio. Table 10 shows service between Pittsburgh and Oil City via New Castle, Mercer, and Stoneboro.

Above: The two-story Victorian style brick, brownstone, and terra cotta Pennsylvania Railroad station at 161 N. 8th Street in the city of Lebanon in Lebanon County, Pennsylvania (also known as the Cornwall and Lebanon Railroad Station) is shown in this postcard view. It was designed by George Watson Hewitt and built in 1885 by the Cornwall and Lebanon Railroad. This railroad opened in 1883 and was acquired by the Pennsylvania Railroad in 1918.

Below: Passengers are at the Pennsylvania Railroad station in the city of Connellsville in Fayette County, Pennsylvania in this postcard postmarked July 10, 1915. Connellsville had passenger service on the Pennsylvania Railroad line from Pittsburgh via Connellsville and Uniontown to Fairchance, Pennsylvania.

Penna. R.R. Station, Emporium, Pa.

Above: No trains can be seen in this quiet moment at the Pennsylvania Railroad station at the borough of Emporium in Cameron County, Pennsylvania in this postcard postmarked April 10, 1907. Emporium was a busy spot where Pennsylvania Railroad passenger service from Buffalo to Philadelphia met the line from Erie to Philadelphia.

Below: Several passengers are ready to board the Pennsylvania Railroad passenger train at the village of Woodville in Sandusky County, Ohio in this postcard scene *c.* 1910. Woodville had a passenger service on the Pennsylvania Railroad line from Pittsburgh, Pennsylvania via Mansfield, Ohio to Toledo, Ohio.

THE SHORTEST RAIL ROUTE BETWEEN THE EAST AND WEST

COACHES ON ALL TRAINS UNLESS OTHERWISE NOTED
PITTSBURGH TO BALTIMORE, WASHINGTON, PHILADELPHIA AND NEW YORK

Miles	Table 53 EASTERN STANDARD TIME	★42 Daily	★2 Dly.	8	★54 Daily	★56-54 Dly.	★72 Dly.	24 Daily	74 Daily	★46-178 Daily	18 Daily	★52 Daily	★16-22 Dly.	★16-580 Daily	★22 Daily	★66 Daily	★50 Daily	★60 Daily	★78 Daily	★36 Daily	36-604 Dly.	★40 Daily	★68 Daily	★68-606 Dly.	★58 Dly.	★48 Night	★28 Night	★30 Night
.0	Lv PITTSBURGH, Pa.	AM 4.22	AM 7.25	AM *8.05	AM 8.30	AM 8.40	AM 9.45	AM 11.05	PM 2.00	PM 4.00	PM 5.00	PM 8.43	PM 9 50	PM 9.50	PM 10.00	1050	PM 10.53	PM 11.00	PM 11.29	PM 11.35	PM 11.35	PM 11.45	PM 12.10	1210	1231	Night 12.41	Night 1.23	Night 1.28

Table continues with intermediate stops: East Liberty, Wilkinsburg, Braddock, East Pittsburgh, Wilmerding, Irwin, Jeannette, Greensburg, Latrobe, Derry, Torrance, Bolivar, New Florence, Johnstown, South Fork, Portage, Cresson, Gallitzin, Horseshoe Curve (Passing Time), Altoona, Bellwood, Tyrone, Huntingdon, Mount Union, Lewistown, Mifflin, Newport, Duncannon, Harrisburg, York, Baltimore, Washington, Middletown, Elizabethtown, Mount Joy, Lancaster, Parkesburg, Coatesville, Downingtown, Frazer, Paoli, Philadelphia (Pa. Sta. 30th St. and Broad St. Station N. Phila.), Atlantic City, Trenton, Princeton Junc., New Brunswick, Elizabeth, Newark, Jersey City (Exchange Place), New York (Hudson Ter., Downtown), New York (Penna. Station), Boston, Mass.

Miles	Station																											
244.7	Ar Harrisburg	10.22	12.50	3.35	1.34	1.41	3.15	7.17	9.42	11.29	2.12	3.20	3.20	3.27	3.59	4.16	4.24	4.29	4.47	4.47	4.53	5.15	5.15	5.34	5.44	6.19	6.30
368.0	Ar WASHINGTON, D.C.	2.00	4.55	8.45	4.55	4.55	8.45	1040	10.40						7.50		8.40	8.40				8.50					9.55
439.3	Ar NEW YORK, N.Y. (Penna. Station)	2.20	4.25	8.40	5.20	5.20	7.00	10.55	11.25	2.35		6.35	7.30		7.30	7.40		8.20	8.05	9.44		8.25	8.55			9.25	9.30	9.50

Note A—At North Phila. Sta. there is a station of the Subway in which trains run frequently to and from City Hall Station at Broad and Market Sts. Running time 12 minutes.

★ Regularly assigned through cars air-conditioned.
* Daily.   † Daily except Sunday.
¶ Daily except Mondays.
⅃ On Sundays leaves Newark 9.14 a. m., arrives Jersey City 9.30 a. m., Hudson Terminal 9.33 a. m.
■ On Sundays leaves Newark 6.21 a. m., arrives Jersey City 6.37 a. m., Hudson Terminal 6.40 a. m.
⊕ On Sundays leaves Newark at 7.32 a. m., arrives Jersey City 7.49 a. m., Hudson Terminal 7.52 a. m.

Reference Notes for Table 53

▲ On Saturdays and Sundays leaves Newark 6.42 p. m., arrives Jersey City 6.58 p. m., Hudson Terminal, 7.01 p. m.
Ψ On Saturdays leaves Newark 9.22 a. m., arrives Jersey City 9.38 a. m., Hudson Terminal 9.41 a. m.
c Stops only to receive passengers.
d Stops only to discharge passengers.
f Stops only on signal or notice to agent or conductor to receive or discharge passengers.

g On Sundays arrives Atlantic City 10.00 a. m.
h Stops only on notice to conductor to discharge passengers from points west of Pittsburgh.
k Saturdays only.
r Stops only on notice to conductor to discharge passengers from points west of Philadelphia.
s Stops Sunday only.
u Hudson & Manhattan R. R. Station.
v New York baggage arrives Boston at 5.00 p. m.

The April 2, 1939 Pennsylvania Railroad timetable shows twenty-four daily eastbound passenger trains from Pittsburgh to Philadelphia. As shown on the timetable, most of the smaller communities along the route also had passenger service. There were about twenty westbound passenger trains from Philadelphia to Pittsburgh.

Left: In this postcard postmarked November 14, 1916, the city of Alliance in Stark County, Ohio is a busy spot on the Pennsylvania Railroad. The Pittsburgh via Alliance, Canton, and Crestline to Fort Wayne line crosses the Cleveland via Alliance and Wellsville to Pittsburgh line here.

Below: Lounges and special facilities are shown in this postcard to make the service men comfortable and provide emotional support for the United States military during the Second World War. These facilities were maintained in a number of Pennsylvania Railroad stations. They were operated by the USO (United Service Organization founded in 1941), the Travelers' Aid, and local patriotic organizations including the Women's Aid of the Pennsylvania Railroad.

Relaxing, USO Lounge, Union Station, Cincinnati, Ohio.

At Ease, USO Lounge, Union Station, Dayton, Ohio.

Reading and Writing, USO Lounge, Union Station, Columbus, Ohio.

At Pennsylvania Railroad Station, Dennison, Ohio, a Popular "Portable Canteen"

Above: A Cumberland Valley Railroad passenger train is at Williams Grove, Pennsylvania in this postcard scene. The May 28, 1916 timetable showed seven trains Monday through Saturday (four on Sunday) from Harrisburg via Williams Grove to Dillsburg and seven trains Monday through Saturday (five on Sunday) from Dillsburg via Williams Grove to Harrisburg. On June 2, 1919, the Cumberland Valley Railroad was officially purchased by the Pennsylvania Railroad.

Below: The Pennsylvania Railroad station at Harrisburg, Pennsylvania is a busy spot in this postcard scene. This station has continued to be an important point on the Amtrak system with the January 14, 2013 timetable showing fourteen trains in each direction Monday through Friday and eight trains in each direction on Saturday and Sunday between Harrisburg and Philadelphia. There is one train daily in each direction between Harrisburg and Pittsburgh.

Above: On October 8, 1946, Pennsylvania Railroad class K4s Pacific type steam locomotive with a 4-6-2 wheel arrangement No. 3670 has arrived at Huntingdon, Pennsylvania with a passenger train. This locomotive was built at the Juniata Shops of the Pennsylvania Railroad in June 1918 and was sold for scrap in August 1955. (*Photograph by Bill Price, Robert Feddersen Collection*)

Below: A Pennsylvania Railroad passenger train headed by class K4s Pacific type steam locomotive No. 623 is at Huntingdon, Pennsylvania on October 7, 1946. This locomotive was built at the Juniata Shops of the Pennsylvania Railroad in July 1917 and was scrapped in May 1948. (*Photograph by Bill Price, Robert Feddersen Collection*)

Above: On August 27, 1953, Pennsylvania Railroad class K4s Pacific type steam locomotive No. 3674 is at the city of Camden in Camden County, New Jersey. This locomotive was built at the Juniata Shops of the Pennsylvania Railroad in June 1918 and was sold for scrap in August 1955. (*Photograph by R. R. Wallin, Robert Feddersen Collection*)

Right: Pennsylvania Railroad passenger train No. 723 (New York via Newark, South Amboy, and Long Branch to Bay Head Junction, New Jersey), powered by class K4s Pacific type steam locomotive No. 5417, is at the city of South Amboy in Middlesex County, New Jersey on August 19, 1954. The locomotive was built by Baldwin Locomotive Works in February 1927 and was sold for scrap in August 1955. (*Photograph by Robert Feddersen*)

Left: South Amboy, New Jersey is the location of train No. 722 (Bay Head Junction, New Jersey via Long Branch, South Amboy, and Newark to New York) headed by class K4s Pacific type steam locomotive No. 3678 on August 18, 1954. The locomotive was built by the Juniata Shops of the Pennsylvania Railroad in April 1918 and was sold for scrap in 1957. (*Photograph by Robert Feddersen*)

Below: Pennsylvania Reading Seashore Lines class K4s Pacific type steam locomotive No. 3806 is at the unincorporated community of Ancora in Camden County, New Jersey (about 2.4 miles from Winslow Junction, New Jersey) on June 27, 1954. The locomotive was built at the Juniata Shops of the Pennsylvania Railroad in March 1923 and was retired in October 1956. (*Craig Knox Collection*)

Above: Class T1 Duplex type steam locomotive with a 4-4-4-4 wheel arrangement No. 5533 was built for the Pennsylvania Railroad by Baldwin Locomotive Works in April 1946 and was retired in December 1953. This was to be a passenger locomotive for long distance trains. These locomotives proved to be so slippery as to be almost uncontrollable. This, together with high maintenance costs resulted in these locomotives being downgraded to local passenger services. (*Craig Knox Collection*)

Below: Pennsylvania Railroad class M1a Mountain type steam locomotive with a 4-8-2 wheel arrangement No. 6740 is ready for the next assignment. This locomotive was built by Baldwin Locomotive Works in June 1930 and was retired in June 1954. (*Craig Knox Collection*)

Left: Electro-Motive Division of General Motors Corporation in April 1949 built 2,000 horsepower type E7A diesel locomotive No. 5883 for the Pennsylvania Railroad. (*Craig Knox Collection*)

Below: Pennsylvania Railroad class GG1 electric locomotive No. 4814 is handling a passenger train on the New York to Washington D.C. corridor. This locomotive, built by the General Electric Company in August 1935, was scrapped in May 1967. The durable GG1 with its unusual shape symbolized the Pennsylvania Railroad. There were 139 GG1 locomotives of which 57 were geared for freight service and 82 were used in passenger service. (*Craig Knox Collection*)

Above: A freight train is powered by class GG1 electric locomotive No. 4920 in the Philadelphia area around 1962. This locomotive was built at the Juniata Shops of the Pennsylvania Railroad with General Electric Company motors and controls in July 1942. It was sold to Amtrak in January 1973 and was renumbered 918. (*Photograph by Craig Knox*)

Below: A Pennsylvania Railroad passenger train comprised of a baggage car and three passenger cars is powered by class K4s Pacific type steam locomotive No. 3884. This locomotive was built at the Juniata Shops of the Pennsylvania Railroad in July 1923 and was retired in May 1956. (*Craig Knox Collection*)

Left: At New York Avenue in Washington D.C., Pennsylvania class GG1 electric locomotives, both a product of the Pennsylvania Railroad Juniata Shops, No. 4877 (built in January 1939 and equipped with Westinghouse Electric and Manufacturing Company motors and controls) and No. 4894 (built in April 1940 equipped with General Electric Company motors and controls) are awaiting the next assignment in 1962. (*Photograph by Craig Knox*)

Below: Pennsylvania Reading Seashore Lines class E2a Atlantic type steam locomotive with a 4-4-2 wheel arrangement No. 6061 is at 4th Street in Ocean City, New Jersey around 1950. (*Craig Knox Collection*)

Above: In 1950 on 4ᵗʰ Street in Ocean City, New Jersey finds Pennsylvania Reading Seashore Lines class G5s Ten Wheeler type steam locomotive with a 4-6-0 wheel arrangement No. 5710. This locomotive was built by the Juniata Shops of the Pennsylvania Railroad in August 1924. It was retired in September 1953. (*Craig Knox Collection*)

Below: Class E6s Atlantic type steam locomotive with a 4-4-2 wheel arrangement No. 1238 is handling a Pennsylvania Reading Seashore Lines passenger train along 10th Street in Ocean City, New Jersey in 1950. This locomotive was built in May 1914 by the Pennsylvania Railroad's Juniata Shops and was retired in April 1951. (*Craig Knox Collection*)

Above: In the 1940s, Pennsylvania Reading Seashore Lines class E6s Atlantic type steam locomotive No. 759 is at 4th Street in Ocean City, New Jersey. This locomotive, built at the Pennsylvania Railroad Juniata Shops in May 1914, was sold for scrap in May 1949. (*Craig Knox Collection*)

Below: On October 22, 1960, the Norristown Local of the Pennsylvania Railroad with two class MP54 electric multiple unit cars is posing for a picture just before entering Norristown, Pennsylvania. This line, which paralleled the Reading Railroad line to Norristown, was electrified on July 20, 1930. (*Photograph by Kenneth C. Springirth*)

Above: The Pennsylvania Railroad two car Norristown Local headed by class MP54E2-TC electric multiple unit car No. 743 (one of 200 cars numbered 619 to 819 built in 1926 to 1930) has arrived at the Haws Avenue Station in the municipality of Norristown in Montgomery County, Pennsylvania on October 22, 1960. (*Photograph by Kenneth C. Springirth*)

Below: The Pennsylvania Railroad storage yard at Haws Avenue in Norristown, Pennsylvania has a weekend lineup of electric multiple unit commuter cars with class MP54E2-TC car No. 723 leading one end of the lineup on October 22, 1960 waiting for the next rush hour assignment. On October 29, 1960, the Pennsylvania Railroad discontinued the commuter service beyond Manayunk to Norristown by the. (*Photograph by Kenneth C. Springirth*)

Left: On March 31, 1961, the class MP54 electric multiple unit two car West Chester local is preparing to leave West Chester, Pennsylvania. This line was built by the West Chester and Philadelphia Railroad which opened from Philadelphia to West Chester on November 18, 1858. In the early 1880s, the Pennsylvania Railroad gained control of the line. (*Photograph by Kenneth C. Springirth*)

Below: It is a quiet March 31, 1961 at West Town station in Chester County, Pennsylvania on the West Chester line of the Pennsylvania Railroad. On January 1, 1983, the Southeastern Pennsylvania Transportation Authority took over this line. (*Photograph by Kenneth C. Springirth*)

Above: Two automobiles
are parked at the Cheney
station on the West Chester
line of the Pennsylvania
Railroad on March 31,
1961. The Southeastern
Pennsylvania Transportation
Authority cut back the line
from West Chester to Elwyn,
Pennsylvania on September
19, 1986. (*Photograph by
Kenneth C. Springirth*)

Right: The impressive
Glen Mills station on the
West Chester line of the
Pennsylvania Railroad
is quietly waiting for the
afternoon rush hour of
March 31, 1961. Currently,
the West Chester Railroad
operates passenger train
excursion service between
West Chester and Glen Mills,
Pennsylvania. (*Photograph by
Kenneth C. Springirth*)

Above: Pennsylvania Railroad box cab class P5 electric locomotive No. 4700 is handling a railroad excursion that is at the Lancaster, Pennsylvania station on April 23, 1961. This locomotive originally numbered 7898 and renumbered to 4700 in September 1933 was built by the Pennsylvania Railroad's Juniata Shops with Westinghouse Electric and Manufacturing Company equipment in July 1931 and was retired in April 1965. (*Photograph by Kenneth C. Springirth*)

Left: On April 23, 1961, at the Lancaster, Pennsylvania train station (which opened in 1929), Pennsylvania Railroad electric locomotive No. 4700 is adorned with a fresh coat of paint making it a photographer's delight. This was one of two experimental class P5 locomotives that were successful and with some minor changes led to the building of class P5a electric locomotives numbered 4701 to 4790 during the years 1932 to 1935. (*Photograph by Kenneth C. Springirth*)

Right: The rail excursion, using Pennsylvania Railroad electric locomotive No. 4700, is eastbound with a photograph stop at Leamon Place in Lancaster County, Pennsylvania near the interchange with the Strasburg Railroad on April 23, 1961. (*Photograph by Kenneth C. Springirth*)

Below: On April 23, 1961, Pennsylvania Railroad class D16sb American type steam locomotive with a 4-4-0 wheel arrangement No. 1223 is on display at the Strasburg Railroad in Strasburg, Pennsylvania. This locomotive was built at the Juniata Shops of the Pennsylvania Railroad in November 1905. The locomotive is now at the Railroad Museum of Pennsylvania located in Strasburg. (*Photograph by Kenneth C. Springirth*)

Left: Pennsylvania Railroad model 660 gas electric doodlebug No. 4666 is on the siding at the city of Trenton in Mercer County, New Jersey on April 20, 1962. This unit was delivered on June 20, 1930 by J. G. Brill Company and had a 415 horsepower Hall-Scott gasoline engine with a top speed of sixty miles per hour on level track with the capability of pulling four fifty-ton trailer cars at forty-three miles per hour on level track. (*Photograph by Kenneth C. Springirth*)

Below: On April 20, 1962, a Pennsylvania Railroad class GG1 electric locomotive No. 4913 is arriving at Trenton, New Jersey with a passenger train. This locomotive was built in January 1942 at the Juniata Shops of the Pennsylvania Railroad and was equipped with Westinghouse Electric and Manufacturing Company motors and General Electric Company controls. It was sold in January 1973 and became Amtrak No. 913. The locomotive is now at the Altoona Railroaders Memorial Museum. (*Photograph by Kenneth C. Springirth*)

Above: Pennsylvania Reading Seashore Lines 1,600 horsepower type AS16 diesel locomotive No. 6010, built in March 1953 by Baldwin Locomotive Works, is bringing a passenger train into the deserted Broadway station in Camden, New Jersey station on June 14, 1962. The Pennsylvania Reading Seashore Lines purchased sixteen of this type of locomotive numbered 6007 to 6016 and 6022 to 6027. (*Photograph by Kenneth C. Springirth*)

Right: On April 14, 1962, Pennsylvania Railroad doodlebug No. 4666 is coming into the Camden, New Jersey station. This is the only survivor of five model 660 gas electric doodlebugs numbered 4666 to 4670 built by J. G. Brill Company in 1920. (*Photograph by Kenneth C. Springirth*)

Left: Pennsylvania Railroad vintage doodlebug No. 4666 is shown with three passenger cars parked to the left of the 1,000 horsepower type DRS4-4-1000 diesel locomotive No. 9277 (built by the Baldwin Locomotive Works in 1949) in the borough of Pemberton located in Burlington County, New Jersey on June 12, 1962. (*Photograph by Kenneth C. Springirth*)

Below: On December 1, 1962, a train of Pennsylvania Railroad, well maintained class MP54 electric multiple unit cars, has arrived at Ellsworth Street heading for the stadium for the Army Navy game in Philadelphia, Pennsylvania. Beginning in 1936, the Pennsylvania Railroad offered special trains from New York City and Washington D.C. that provided passengers with magnificient direct service to the stadium gates for an easy and worry free departure after the game. (*Photograph by Kenneth C. Springirth*)

Right: Pennsylvania Railroad trains are at the Philadelphia Stadium yard on December 1, 1962. Electric locomotive class GG1 No. 4929 is parked at section A. This locomotive, equipped with Westinghouse Electric and Manufacturing Company motors and controls, was built by the Juniata Shops of the Pennsylvania Railroad in February 1943 and was sold in January 1973 becoming Amtrak No. 923. Another train with a class GG1 locomotive is coming into section B. (*Photograph by Kenneth C. Springirth*)

Below: To the left of Pennsylvania Railroad class MP54 electric multiple unit commuter cars is class GG1 electric locomotive No. 4913 at the Philadelphia Stadium yard on December 1, 1962. The Pennsylvania Railroad was famous for providing numerous trains handling thousands of people for the Army-Navy game. (*Photograph by Kenneth C. Springirth*)

Above: On December 1, 1962, Pennsylvania Railroad type E8A diesel locomotives Nos. 5894 (built in 1951), 5798 (built in 1952), and 5797 (built in 1952) are powering a passenger train near Ellsworth Street in Philadelphia heading for the Stadium yard. Each of these locomotives was built by the Electro-Motive Division of General Motors Corporation and was rated at 2,250 horsepower. (*Photograph by Kenneth C. Springirth*)

Left: Pennsylvania Railroad class GG1 electric locomotive No. 4937 is at Ellsworth Street in Philadelphia on December 1, 1962. This locomotive, equipped with Westinghouse Electric and Manufacturing Company motors and controls, was built by the Juniata Shops of the Pennsylvania Railroad in February 1943 and was sold in January 1973 becoming Amtrak No. 923. (*Photograph by Kenneth C. Springirth*)

Right: Pennsylvania Railroad type E8A diesel locomotive No. 5894 (built by Electro-Motive Division of General Motors Corporation) and electric locomotive class GG1 No. 4918 (equipped with General Electric Company motors and controls and built by the Juniata Shops of the Pennsylvania Railroad in June 1942) are at the Philadelphia Stadium yard on December 1, 1962. Locomotive No. 4918 was sold in January 1973 becoming Amtrak No. 916. (*Photograph by Kenneth C. Springirth*)

Below: Sharp looking Pennsylvania Railroad class GG1 electric locomotive No. 4884 is at the Philadelphia Stadium yard on December 1, 1962. This locomotive, equipped with General Electric Company motors and controls, was built by the Juniata Shops of the Pennsylvania Railroad in March 1939. For the Army-Navy game, the railroad repaired and cleaned cars, locomotives were washed and polished, and extra personnel were on hand to assure a smooth operation. (*Photograph by Kenneth C. Springirth*)

Above: Pennsylvania Railroad electric multiple unit commuter cars are in position at the Philadelphia Stadium yard at section K for the Army–Navy game on December 1, 1962. In 1941 a record forty-two trains arrived at the game. That was reduced to 29 in 1954, 18 in 1962, and four in the last year of that service in 1975. (*Photograph by Kenneth C. Springirth*)

Left: Class MP54E2-TC Pennsylvania Railroad electric multiple unit car No. 725 is leading a train at Ellsworth Street in Philadelphia heading for the Stadium yard bringing passengers to the Army–Navy game on December 1, 1962. The last year of this special service was in 1975. (*Photograph by Kenneth C. Springirth*)

Above: On May 23, 1964, the Pennsylvania Railroad *Southern Express*, powered by 2,250 horsepower type E8A diesel locomotive No. 5904 built in 1951 by the Electro-Motive Division of General Motors Corporation, is in a rural area just south of Erie, Pennsylvania on its trip to Philadelphia. (*Photograph by Kenneth C. Springirth*)

Below: The Pennsylvania Railroad train No. 581 *Northern Express* headed by 2,000 horsepower type E7A diesel locomotive No. 5861 built in 1948 by the Electro-Motive Division of General Motors Corporation is passing though Corry, Pennsylvania on its trip to Erie, Pennsylvania in November 1964. Passenger service from Erie to Philadelphia ended when train No. 580 made its last run on March 27, 1965. (*Photograph by Michael B. Shannon*)

Above: A southbound passenger train powered by Pennsylvania Railroad class GG1 electric locomotive No. 4935 is passing Curtis Park station in the borough of Sharon Hill in Delaware County, Pennsylvania in January 1967. This locomotive, equipped with General Electric Company motors and Westinghouse Electric and Manufacturing Company controls, was built at the Juniata Shops of the Pennsylvania Railroad in March 1943. (*Photograph by James A. Gillin*)

Left: On September 2, 1968, Penn Central Transportation Company class GG1 electric locomotive No. 4878 is powering an eastbound passenger train through Paoli in Chester County, Pennsylvania. This locomotive, equipped with General Electric Company motors and controls, was built at the Juniata Shops of the Pennsylvania Railroad in February 1939. The Pennsylvania Railroad and New York Central Railroad merged on February 1, 1968 into the Penn Central Transportation Company. (*Photograph by Kenneth C. Springirth*)

Right: Penn Central Transportation Company class GG1 No. 4914 is at 30th Street Station in Philadelphia on August 31, 1968. This locomotive, equipped with General Electric Company motors and controls, was built at the Juniata Shops of the Pennsylvania Railroad in June 1942 and was sold in January 1973 becoming Amtrak No. 914. (*Photograph by Kenneth C. Springirth*)

Below: On August 31, 1968, Penn Central Transportation Company class GG1 No. 4932 is leaving 30th Street Station in Philadelphia. This locomotive, equipped with General Electric Company motors and controls, was built at the Juniata Shops of the Pennsylvania Railroad in February 1943 and was sold in January 1973 becoming Amtrak No. 925. (*Photograph by Kenneth C. Springirth*)

Left: A westbound Penn Central Transportation Company passenger train has pulled into the station at Harrisburg, Pennsylvania on September 2, 1968 powered by type E8A diesel locomotives (still in the Pennsylvania Railroad paint scheme) No. 4258 (built as No. 5798 in June 1952) and No. 4319 (built as No. 5839 in February 1951) built by the Electro-Motive Division of General Motors Corporation for the Pennsylvania Railroad. (*Photograph by Kenneth C. Springirth*)

Below: At Harrisburg, Pennsylvania on September 2, 1968, Penn Central Transportation Company (formerly Pennsylvania Railroad class GG1) electric locomotives No. 4878 (built in February 1939 and equipped with General Electric Company motors and controls) and No. 4870 (built in December 1938 and equipped with Westinghouse Electric and Manufacturing Company motors and controls) are waiting for the next assignment. Both locomotives were built at the Juniata Shops of the Pennsylvania Railroad. (*Photograph by Kenneth C. Springirth*)

Right: With a light dusting of snow on the ground, Penn Central Transportation Company class GG1 electric locomotive No. 4920 is at Harrisburg, Pennsylvania on December 27, 1970. This locomotive, built at the Juniata Shops of the Pennsylvania Railroad with General Electric Company motors and controls in July 1942, was sold in January 1973 and became Amtrak No. 918. (*Photograph by Kenneth C. Springirth*)

Below: Penn Central Transportation Company 2,250 horsepower type E8A diesel No. 4314, is at Harrisburg, Pennsylvania on December 27, 1970. This locomotive was originally built by the Electro-Motive Division of General Motors Corporation in October 1952 as number 5714A for the Pennsylvania Railroad. (*Photograph by Kenneth C. Springirth*)

Above: On December 27, 1970, at the Penn Central Transportation Company yard in Paoli, Pennsylvania, electric multiple unit commuter cars vintage class MP54 is on the left and Silverliner II (named because of the shiny stainless steel body) No. 204 is on the right. Between 1963 and 1964 the Budd Company built 38 Silverliner II cars for the Pennsylvania Railroad numbered 201 to 219 and 251 to 269. (*Photograph by Kenneth C. Springirth*)

Left: At Harrisburg, Pennsylvania on a cold December 27, 1970 Penn Central Transportation Company class GG1 electric locomotive No. 4851 is ready for service. This locomotive, equipped with Westinghouse Electric and Manufacturing Company motors and controls, was built at the Juniata Shops of the Pennsylvania Railroad in June 1935. (*Photograph by Kenneth C. Springirth*)

Above: On August 1, 1977, at Harrisburg, Pennsylvania are class GG1 electric locomotives built at the Juniata Shops of the Pennsylvania Railroad and sold to Amtrak in January 1973: No. 925 (originally No. 4932 equipped with General Electric Company motors and controls, built in February 1943), No. 4933 (equipped with Westinghouse Electric and Manufacturing Company motors and controls built in March 1943), No. 900 (originally No. 4892 equipped with General Electric Company motors and controls built in March 1940, and No. 917 (originally No. 4919 equipped with Westinghouse Electric and Manufacturing Company motors and controls built in July 1942). (*Photograph by Kenneth C. Springirth*)

Right: Consolidated Rail Corporation two-car train of electric multiple unit Silverliner II commuter cars headed by No. 260 (built by the Budd Company) is at the borough of Elizabethtown in Lancaster County, Pennsylvania in April 1977. On April 1, 1976, Penn Central Transportation Company along with a number of railroads were merged into the Consolidated Rail Corporation. (*Photograph by Kenneth C. Springirth*)

Above: On October 7, 2001, former Pennsylvania Railroad type E8A diesel locomotives No. 5711 (built in October 1952) and No. 5809 (built in January 1951), restored by the Juniata Terminal Company (a locomotive leasing and railcar storage company headed by Bennett Levin) are at the crest of the Horseshoe Curve westbound from Altoona to Gallitzin, Pennsylvania. This curve is about 1,300 feet across at its widest point. As a train travels west from Altoona, it climbs almost 60 feet in the 0.7 mile segment that makes up the curve. (*Photograph by Donald A. Woshlo, Jr.*)

Below: Eastbound from Gallitzin to Altoona, Pennsylvania, former Pennsylvania Railroad diesel locomotives No. 5711 and No. 5809 (both built by Electro-Motive Division of General Motors Corporation) are at the Horseshoe Curve on October 7, 2001. An observation park for visitors was completed in 1879, and in the 1990s, a visitor center was constructed. (*Photograph by Donald A. Woshlo, Jr.*)

CHAPTER 3

RAILROADS SERVING THE FORMER PENNSYLVANIA RAILROAD

Amtrak began passenger train operation on May 1, 1971. Following the June 1, 1970 bankruptcy of the Penn Central Transportation Company, the United States Congress passed the Railroad Revitalization and Regulatory Reform Act of 1976 which enabled the transfer of portions of the Northeast Corridor, not already owned by state authorities, to Amtrak. That former Pennsylvania Railroad route from Boston to Washington D.C. became Amtrak's busiest line which for the year ending September 2012 carried 11.4 million of Amtrak's total of 31.2 million passengers. The former Pennsylvania Railroad line from New York via Philadelphia to Pittsburgh has one daily Amtrak train in each direction. However, the portion between New York via Philadelphia and Harrisburg has numerous passenger trains.

The Norfolk Southern Railway began with the formation of the Norfolk and Western Railway in 1881. On October 16, 1964, the Nickel Plate Road merged into the Norfolk and Western Railway. The Norfolk and Western Railway and Southern Railway merged to become the Norfolk Southern Railway on December 31, 1990.

When Consolidated Rail Corporation, which on April 1, 1976 took over the bankrupt Penn Central Transportation Company and several other ailing railroads, became profitable, CSX Transportation and Norfolk Southern Railway both submitted bids to buy it. On June 23, 1997 Norfolk Southern Railway and CSX Transportation submitted a joint application to purchase, divide and operate Consolidated Rail Corporation. Norfolk Southern acquired 58 percent and CSX Transportation acquired 42 percent of the former assets of Consolidated Rail Corporation and began train operation over those lines on June 1, 1999. Most of the surviving Pennsylvania Railroad route structure was acquired by Norfolk Southern Railway. The former Pennsylvania Railroad mainline between Pittsburgh and Harrisburg is now operated by Norfolk Southern Railway.

The former Pennsylvania Railroad line from Tyrone via Milesburg to Lock Haven and from Milesburg via Bellefonte to Pleasant Gap and Lemont in Pennsylvania is now operated by the Nittany and Bald Eagle Railroad. The Tyrone and Lock Haven Railroad was incorporated in 1857 and became the Bald Eagle Valley Railroad in 1861. It was acquired by the Pennsylvania Railroad in 1861. Some of the trackage was abandoned by Consolidated Rail Corporation in 1982 and 1983. On August 1, 1984, the Nittany and Bald Eagle Railroad was established and today hauls stone, general merchandise, and serves as a bridge line to move coal to power plants.

On April 1, 1954, the Everett Railroad began operation on a four mile section of the abandoned Huntingdon and Broad Top Railroad. Freight business was declining and passenger excursion service was operated from 1965 to 1968. When Consolidated Rail Corporation abandoned its interchange, the Everett Railroad was abandoned in 1982, but under new ownership in 1985 leased seventeen miles of track between Hollidaysburg, Roaring Spring, Martinsburg, and Curryville, Pennsylvania. This was a former Pennsylvania Railroad line that operated from Altoona via Hollidaysburg, Roaring Spring, Martinsburg, and Henrietta.

Northwest of Pittsburgh, Pennsylvania, the Kiski Junction Railroad operates over a portion of the former Pennsylvania Railroad. The Allegheny Valley Railroad was opened from Pittsburgh via Schenley to Kittanning, Pennsylvania on January 30, 1856 and was leased to the Pennsylvania Railroad on July 31, 1900. It became the main line of the Pennsylvania Railroad from Pittsburgh to Buffalo. Under Consolidated Rail Corporation, all but 5.2 miles of line was sold off in 1992. In 1995, the Kiski Junction Railroad bought the 5.2-mile active freight line. Today the Kiski Junction Railroad operates from the bridge over the Kiskiminetas River (that was built in 1899 and is the interchange point with the Norfolk Southern Railway) through Schenley via a restored nine-mile line to the Rosebud Mining Company Logansport Mine. Norfolk Southern Railway operates coal trains to serve the mine. In addition, the Kiski Junction Railroad operates from Schenley to Bagdad for freight service and passenger service over the former Pennsylvania Railroad line from Pittsburgh via Freeport and Bagdad to Blairsville.

Left: An eastbound Amtrak train to Philadelphia is arriving at the borough of Middletown in Dauphin County, Pennsylvania on April 14, 2002 with 4,250 horsepower type P42 diesel locomotive No. 102 built by the General Electric Company at the head end. (*Photograph by Kenneth C. Springirth*)

Below: Eastbound Amtrak train No. 42 the *Pennsylvanian* is loading passengers at Lewistown Junction, Pennsylvania on October 13, 2011 headed by 4,250 horsepower type P42 diesel locomotive No. 24 built by the General Electric Company. This station, opened in 1849 as a freight station and converted to passenger use in 1868, is the oldest surviving structure known to have been built by the Pennsylvania Railroad. (*Photograph by Kenneth C. Springirth*)

Above: Westbound Amtrak train No. 43 the *Pennsylvanian* is coming into Lewistown Junction, Pennsylvania on April 30, 2012 powered by 4,250 horsepower type P42 locomotive No. 117 built by the General Electric Company. Regularly scheduled stage coach trips began in 1786 between Philadelphia and Pittsburgh requiring three weeks. In 2013, making numerous stops the *Pennsylvanian* covers that distance in about seven-and-a-half hours. (*Photograph by Kenneth C. Springirth*)

Below: On March 17, 2013, eastbound Amtrak train the *Pennsylvanian* is at Lewistown Junction, Pennsylvania headed by 3,200 horsepower type P32-8 diesel locomotive No. 512 built by General Electric Company in 1991. The Pennsylvania Railroad Technical and Historical Society purchased the station in 1985 and renovated it for their research center. In addition to maintaining the building and grounds, society members open and close the waiting room for Amtrak passengers. (*Photograph by Kenneth C. Springirth*)

Left: Tyrone, Pennsylvania on July 12, 2013, is the location of eastbound Amtrak train No. 42 the *Pennsylvanian* powered by General Electric built diesel locomotives 3,200 horsepower type P32-8 No. 514 and 4,250 horsepower type P42 No. 152. Tyrone (with 3,108 boardings and alightings for the year ending September 2012) is a flag stop for the *Pennsylvanian* which operates daily once per day in each direction. (*Photograph by Kenneth C. Springirth*)

Below: On a sunny May 14, 2013, eastbound Amtrak train No. 42 the *Pennsylvanian* is at the city of Altoona in Blair County, Pennsylvania with 4,250 horsepower type P42 locomotive No. 160 built by the General Electric Company at the head end as seen from the overhead pedestrian bridge. Altoona had 26,978 boardings and alightings for the year ending September 2012. (*Photograph by Kenneth C. Springirth*)

Right: The eastbound Amtrak train the *Pennsylvanian* on April 28, 2013 is at the Amtrak station in Harrisburg, Pennsylvania headed by 4,250 horsepower type P42 locomotive No. 160 built by the General Electric Company. From Pittsburgh to Harrisburg, the *Pennsylvanian* operates on Norfolk Southern Railway trackage and from Harrisburg to Philadelphia and New York it operates on Amtrak trackage. (*Photograph by Kenneth C. Springirth*)

Below: From left to right Amtrak electric locomotive No. 947 (7,000 horsepower originally built as a type AEM7 by Electro-Motive Division of General Motors Corporation with some parts designed in Sweden by ASEA and rebuilt as type AEM7AC by Amtrak/Alstom) and diesel locomotive No. 119 (4,250 horsepower type P42 built by General Electric Company) are at the Harrisburg, Pennsylvania station on April 28, 2013. (*Photograph by Kenneth C. Springirth*)

Above: On September 28, 2012, Kiski Junction Railroad four axle 1,500 horsepower type GP7R (rebuilt) diesel locomotive No. 752 built originally in March 1951 by the Electro-Motive Division of General Motors Corporation for the Chicago and Northwestern Railway is on the siding at the community of Schenley in Armstrong County, Pennsylvania. This railroad handles freight plus runs scenic passenger excursions. (*Photograph by Kenneth C. Springirth*)

Below: The Kiski Junction Railroad truck, equipped to operate on rail, is making a track inspection of the line from Schenley and has arrived at Bagdad, Pennsylvania on October 14, 2012. Passenger excursion trains are operated between Schenley and Bagdad. (*Photograph by Kenneth C. Springirth*)

Above: On October 14, 2012, Kiski Junction Railroad 600 horsepower type S1 diesel locomotive No. 7135, built by American Locomotive Company in May 1943, is passing Norfolk Southern Railway 4,400 horsepower type ES44AC diesel locomotive No. 8060 (built by General Electric Company in December 2010) with a coal train on the siding at Schenley, Pennsylvania. This coal is used by power plants to generate electricity. (*Photograph by Kenneth C. Springirth*)

Right: The Kiski Junction Railroad excursion train powered by diesel locomotive No. 7135 is approaching Bagdad, Pennsylvania on a beautiful October 14, 2012. At Bagdad, the Kiski Junction Railroad provides freight service to the Allegheny Ludlum metal processing plant. The railroad interchanges with the Norfolk Southern Railway at Kiski Junction on the south side of the Kiskiminetas River across from Schenley. (*Photograph by Kenneth C. Springirth*)

Above: On October 14, 2012, amid the scenic hills around Bagdad, Pennsylvania, Kiski Junction Railroad diesel locomotive No. 7135 shows its neat appearance. This was one of two type S1 diesel locomotives numbered 7135 and 7136 built for the U.S. Army in May 1943 by the American Locomotive Company. (*Photograph by Kenneth C. Springirth*)

Left: An end view of the Kiski Junction Railroad excursion train on October 14, 2012 shows the attractive caboose that is fun to ride. The Kiski Junction Railroad is playing a key role in preserving Pennsylvania's important railroad heritage. (*Photograph by Kenneth C. Springirth*)

Above: A westbound steam excursion using steam locomotive No. 765 (built by the Lima Locomotive Works on September 8, 1944 as a class S2 Berkshire type steam locomotive with a 2-8-4 wheel arrangement for the Nickel Plate Road) is powering the train through the double track Allegheny Tunnel at Gallitzin, Pennsylvania on May 25, 2013 on the former main line of the Pennsylvania Railroad which is now operated by the Norfolk Southern Railway. On the left is the abandoned Gallitzin Tunnel. (*Photograph by Kenneth C. Springirth*)

Right: Steam locomotive No. 765 (now owned by the Fort Wayne Railroad Historical Society) went around the turn around at the borough of Gallitzin in Cambria County, Pennsylvania and is now heading east ready to pass under the Main Street bridge in Gallitzin on May 25, 2013. Back on May 4, 1963, No. 765 was placed on display in Fort Wayne, Indiana. In 1975, work began to restore the locomotive for operation, and on September 1, 1979, No. 765 moved under its own power. (*Photograph by Kenneth C. Springirth*)

Left: At the Main Street bridge in Gallitzin, Pennsylvania on May 25, 2013, Norfolk Southern Railway 4,400 horsepower type ES44AC diesel locomotives No. 8102 in a Pennsylvania Railroad paint scheme and No. 8098 in a Consolidated Rail Corporation paint scheme, both built in February 2012 by the General Electric Company, are backup units for steam locomotive No. 765. (*Photograph by Kenneth C. Springirth*)

Below: On a beautiful May 25, 2013, the eastbound excursion with steam locomotive No. 765 is at the Altoona, Pennsylvania Amtrak station on the Norfolk Southern Railway line. In 1993, No. 765 entered the shop to be completely overhauled, and in 2006 a series of runs were made to verify that the locomotive was road worthy, fully operational, and ready for service. (*Photograph by Kenneth C. Springirth*)

Above: The eastbound Amtrak passenger train the *Pennsylvanian* is approaching the station at the borough of Tyrone in Blair County, Pennsylvania on May 27, 2013 powered by 3,200 horsepower type P32-8 locomotive No. 512. This was one of twenty locomotives numbered 500 to 519 of this type built by General Electric Company in 1991 for Amtrak. (*Photograph by Kenneth C. Springirth*)

Below: Eastbound Amtrak train the *Pennsylvanian* meets the westbound steam excursion with locomotive No. 765 at Tyrone, Pennsylvania on May 27, 2013 on the former mainline of the Pennsylvania Railroad now operated by the Norfolk Southern Railway. To the right of Amtrak locomotive No. 512 is the Tyrone History Museum of the Tyrone Area Historical Society designed to look like a train station. The nearby Tyrone Amtrak station is a simple transit shelter. (*Photograph by Kenneth C. Springirth*)

Above: At the tail end of the eastbound Amtrak train, the *Pennsylvanian*, leaving Tyrone, Pennsylvania on May 27, 2013 is the former New York Central Railroad observation car 'Hickory Creek' (built in 1948 by the Pullman Standard Car Manufacturing Company). This car was christened in Grand Central Terminal in September 15, 1948 and operated on the *Twentieth Century Limited* until it was retired in 1967. It later served the Ringling Brothers and Barnum and Bailey Circus, and has been restored for train travel. (*Photograph by Kenneth C. Springirth*)

Below: The westbound Norfolk Southern Railway steam excursion with steam locomotive No. 765 is passing through Tyrone, Pennsylvania on May 27, 2013. Left of the locomotive is the Tyrone Amtrak station platform. In 2012, the Norfolk Southern Railway leased No. 765 to operate a series of employee specials to mark the railroad's thirtieth anniversary. (*Photograph by Kenneth C. Springirth*)

Right: On May 27, 2013, the westbound Norfolk Southern Railway steam excursion with steam locomotive No. 765 on the former Pennsylvania Railroad mainline is passing under the Jackson Street bridge in Gallitzin, Pennsylvania. In 2013, No. 765 was officially included in the Norfolk Southern Railway program to celebrate the railroad's heritage through steam locomotive operations. (*Photograph by Kenneth C. Springirth*)

Below: East of the Main Street bridge parallel to Portage Street in Gallitzin, Pennsylvania finds the steam excursion train with locomotive No. 765 has used the turnaround and is now heading eastbound on May 27, 2013. The May 2013 Memorial Day Weekend marked the first public steam locomotive excursions over the Horseshoe Curve since 1977. (*Photograph by Kenneth C. Springirth*)

Above: An eastbound Norfolk Southern Railway freight train powered by 3,000 horsepower locomotives No. 6323 (originally type SD50 built in November 1983 and rebuilt as type SD40E in April 2010) and No. 6319 (originally type SD50 built in May 1984 and rebuilt as type SD40E in October 2009) is passing under the pedestrian crosswalk serving the Amtrak station in Altoona, Pennsylvania on March 15, 2013. (*Photograph by Kenneth C. Springirth*)

Below: On March 15, 2013, an eastbound Norfolk Southern Railway coal train, headed by 4,300 horsepower type SD70ACe diesel locomotives built by the Electro-Motive Division of General Motors Corporation No. 1002 (built February 2011) and No. 1059 (built October 2011), is about to pass under the 12th Street pedestrian bridge in Altoona, Pennsylvania with the Amtrak station shelter shown in the upper right of the view. (*Photograph by Kenneth C. Springirth*)

Above: An eastbound Norfolk Southern Railway freight train on the former Pennsylvania Railroad mainline is passing under the pedestrian bridge known as the Cassandra Overlook in the borough of Cassandra in Cambria County, Pennsylvania on October 13, 2012 powered by type Dash 9-40CW diesel locomotives built by General Electric Company No. 9836, built in March 2004, and No. 9667, built in March 2001. (*Photograph by Kenneth C. Springirth*)

Below: On the Rockville bridge over the Susquehanna River north of Harrisburg, Pennsylvania, finds a westbound Norfolk Southern Railway freight train with type Dash 9-40CW diesel locomotive, built in October 2004 by the General Electric Company, No. 9932 at the head end on April 30, 2012. (*Photograph by Kenneth C. Springirth*)

Left: Norfolk Southern Railway 3,000 horsepower helper diesel locomotives No. 6304 (originally type SD50 built in July 1984 and rebuilt as type SD40E in January 2009) and 6319 (originally type SD50 built in May 1984 and rebuilt as type SD40E in October 2009) are traveling on the Horseshoe Curve on April 14, 2012. The 3,500 horsepower SD50 was rebuilt into a 3,000 horsepower SD40E by Norfolk Southern Railway. (*Photograph by Kenneth C. Springirth*)

Below: On April 14, 2012, three Norfolk Southern Railway type Dash 9-40CW diesel locomotives built by General Electric Company No. 9830 (built in March 2004), No. 9707 (built in December 2001), and No. 9851 (built in March 2004) are handling a freight train over the Horseshoe Curve. (*Photograph by Kenneth C. Springirth*)

Above: Rounding the curve at Tyrone, Pennsylvania is Norfolk Southern Railway type Dash 9-40CW diesel locomotive No. 9194, built by General Electric Company in March 1998, is powering a westbound freight train on October 22, 2011. On the left is the well maintained Tyrone History Museum of the Tyrone Area Historical Society. (*Photograph by Kenneth C. Springirth*)

Right: Norfolk Southern Railway type Dash 9-40CW diesel locomotives built by General Electric Company No. 9414, built in February 2000, and No. 8901, built in January 1996, lead a westbound freight train through Tyrone, Pennsylvania on May 14, 2013. (*Photograph by Kenneth C. Springirth*)

Above: At Lewistown Junction, Pennsylvania, Norfolk Southern Railway built by General Electric Company type Dash 9-40CW diesel locomotive No. 9627 (built in February 2001) and type Dash 8-40CW No. 8350 (built in March 1991) are passing by with a coal train on October 13, 2011.   (*Photograph by Kenneth C. Springirth*)

Below: On May 27, 2013, Norfolk Southern Railway 4,000 horsepower type ES40DC diesel locomotive No. 7556 (built by General Electric Company in February 2006) and 4,000 horsepower type SD70M-2 (built by Electro-Motive Division of General Motors Corporation in February 2006) No. 2721 are leading a freight train by Grant Street in the borough of Lilly in Cambria County, Pennsylvania.   (*Photograph by Kenneth C. Springirth*)

Above: Norfolk Southern Railway 3,800 horsepower type SD60I diesel locomotives No. 6719 (built November 1994), No. 6740 (built April 1995), and No. 6726 (built November 1994) all built by the Electro-Motive Division of General Motors Corporation are powering an eastbound coal train as seen from the Pennsylvania Highway 53 bridge going over the tracks east of Cresson, Pennsylvania on May 27, 2013. (*Photograph by Kenneth C. Springirth*)

Below: The rear pusher Norfolk Southern Railway 3,000 horsepower locomotives No. 6312 (originally type SD50 built in December 1983 and rebuilt as type SD40E in February 2009) and No. 6303 (originally type SD50 built in July 1984 and rebuilt as type SD40E in November 2008) of the eastbound coal train headed by locomotives Nos. 6719, 6740, and 6726 (shown in the above picture) have just passed under the Pennsylvania Highway 53 bridge east of Cresson, Pennsylvania on May 27, 2013. (*Photograph by Kenneth C. Springirth*)

Left: On May 25, 2013, an eastbound Norfolk Southern Railway freight train powered by diesel locomotives No. 6322 (originally type SD50 built in June 1984 and rebuilt as type SD40E in March 2010), plus type 9-40CW built by General Electric Company No. 9094 (built April 1997), and 9480 (built April 2000) is ready to enter the Allegheny Tunnel. On the left is the abandoned Gallitzin Tunnel. (*Photograph by Kenneth C. Springirth*)

Below: Norfolk Southern Railway 4,300 horsepower type SD70Ace diesel locomotives built in October 2011 by the Electro-Motive Division of General Motors Corporation No. 1045 and No. 1064 are coming through the double track Allegheny Tunnel at Gallitzin, Pennsylvania with a westbound freight train on May 27, 2013. (*Photograph by Kenneth C. Springirth*)

Right: A westbound Norfolk Southern Railway freight train is passing through the borough of Cresson in Cambria County, Pennsylvania on April 30, 2013 powered by 5,000 horsepower type SD80MAC diesel locomotives built by the Electro-Motive Division of General Motors Corporation No. 7216 (built July 1995), No. 7212 (built April 1996), and No. 7215 (built May 1996). These diesel locomotives were originally delivered to Consolidated Rail Corporation, and when it was split up, Norfolk Southern Railway received seventeen units numbered 7200 to 7216. (*Photograph by Kenneth C. Springirth*)

Below: On May 25, 2013, Norfolk Southern Railway diesel locomotives 5,000 horsepower type SD80MAC diesel locomotive No. 7216 (built in July 1995 by the Electro-Motive Division of General Motors Corporation) and No. 6302 (originally type SD50 built in July 1984 and rebuilt as 3,000 horsepower type SD40E in August 2008) are at the Cresson, Pennsylvania engine terminal waiting for the next assignment. (*Photograph by Kenneth C. Springirth*)

Above: Here is a view of Norfolk Southern Railway diesel locomotives 4,000 horsepower type Dash 8-40C No. 8689 built in December 1990 and type 9-40CW No. 9789 built in May 2003 (both built by the General Electric Company) at Enola Yard on April 28, 2012 taken from U.S. Highway 15. (*Photograph by Kenneth C. Springirth*)

Left: Harrisburg, Pennsylvania near the Harrisburg Transportation Center is the scene for Norfolk Southern Railway type Dash 9-40CW diesel locomotive No. 9217 built in April 1998 by the General Electric Company leading a westbound freight train on April 28, 2013. (*Photograph by Kenneth C. Springirth*)

Above: On October 24, 2009, North Shore Railroad (parent company of the Nittany and Bald Eagle Railroad) 1,200 horsepower type SW9 diesel switcher locomotive No. 446 (originally built as No. 8983 for the New York Central Railroad by the Electro-Motive Division of General Motors Corporation in January 1953) is at one end of the special excursion train being operated by the Nittany and Bald Eagle Railroad for the Bellefonte Historical Railroad at High Street in the Bellefonte, Pennsylvania. (*Photograph by Kenneth C. Springirth*)

Below: A passenger excursion from Bellefonte, Pennsylvania over the former Pennsylvania Railroad is coming down Washington Avenue ready to cross West 12th Street in Tyrone, Pennsylvania powered by Nittany and Bald Eagle Railroad diesel locomotive No. 1602 on October 22, 2011. This special train made a rest stop at the Tyrone History Museum of the Tyrone Area Historical Society before returning to Bellefonte. (*Photograph by Kenneth C. Springirth*)

Above: Nittany and Bald Eagle Railroad diesel locomotive No. 1603 is awaiting departure time at the bridge over the Little Juniata River in Tyrone, Pennsylvania on October 22, 2011 for the return trip to Bellefonte, Pennsylvania. Locomotive No. 1602 was at the other end of the train operated for the Bellefonte Historical Railroad. This is north of the interchange point with the Norfolk Southern Railway. (*Photograph by Kenneth C. Springirth*)

Left: Northbound on Washington Avenue as it approaches West 11th Street in Tyrone, Pennsylvania finds Nittany and Bald Eagle Railroad 1,500 horsepower rebuilt type GP8 diesel locomotive No. 1603 (built originally as type GP7 No. 634 for the Reading Railroad in October 1953 by the Electro-Motive Division of General Motors Corporation) handling a Bellefonte Historical Railroad excursion train for the return trip to Bellefonte, Pennsylvania on October 22, 2011. (*Photograph by Kenneth C. Springirth*)

Above: Nittany and Bald Eagle Railroad 1,500 horsepower rebuilt type GP8 diesel locomotive No. 1602 (built originally as type GP7 No. 5614 for the Peoria and Eastern Railway in November 1950 by the Electro-Motive Division of General Motors Corporation) is on the rear of the northbound Bellefonte Historical Railroad excursion train as it proceeds along former Pennsylvania Railroad trackage on Washington Avenue at West 11th Street in Tyrone, Pennsylvania on October 22, 2011. (*Photograph by Kenneth C. Springirth*)

Below: Pennsylvania Railroad baggage car No. 1951 and Pennsylvania Railroad dining car No. 1957 'Chillisquaque Creek' are on the special train at Bellefonte, Pennsylvania ready to make an excursion to Tyrone, Pennsylvania via the Nittany and Bald Eagle Railroad on October 21, 2012. The Pennsylvania Railroad began operating the Bald Eagle Valley Railroad from Tyrone to Milesburg and Bellefonte on January 1, 1863. The railroad was completed from Milesburg to Lock Haven, Pennsylvania on December 1, 1864. (*Photograph by Kenneth C. Springirth*)

Above: On October 21, 2012, Nittany and Bald Eagle Railroad diesel locomotive No. 1602 with former Pennsylvania Railroad caboose No. 478044 are awaiting departure time at the borough of Bellefonte in Centre County, Pennsylvania for the Bellefonte Historical Railroad excursion train to Tyrone, Pennsylvania. (*Photograph by Kenneth C. Springirth*)

Left: The Bellefonte Historical Railroad excursion is pulling into Tyrone, Pennsylvania on October 21, 2012 powered by Nittany and Bald Eagle Railroad diesel locomotive No. 1602. By railroad, Tyrone was about halfway between Harrisburg and Pittsburgh, and it became an important shipping center, plus a busy stop on the Pennsylvania Railroad between Philadelphia and Pittsburgh. (*Photograph by Kenneth C. Springirth*)

Left: On April 30, 2012, Juniata Valley Railroad 900 horsepower type SW900 diesel switcher locomotive No. 2106 (built originally as a type SW9 in November 1953 by the Electro-Motive Division of General Motors Corporation) is switching a tank car at Lewistown Junction, Pennsylvania. The Juniata Valley Railroad operates eleven miles of former Pennsylvania Railroad track serving Lewistown, Maitland, and Burnham plus interchanges with the Norfolk Southern Railway at Lewistown Junction. (*Photograph by Kenneth C. Springirth*)

Below: At Lewistown Junction, Pennsylvania, on April 30, 2012, Juniata Valley diesel locomotive No. 2106 is handling switching duties. This former Pennsylvania Railroad line became Penn Central Transportation Company. When Consolidated Rail Corporation decided to abandon the line in 1996, the Juniata Valley Railroad came into existence to operate the freight service. (*Photograph by Kenneth C. Springirth*)

Left: Everett Railroad diesel locomotive No. 1712 is handling a passenger excursion at Roaring Spring, Pennsylvania on October 13, 2012. Locomotive No. 1712 (originally built by the Electro-Motive Division of General Motors Corporation for the Clinchfield Railroad as a type GP7 No. 911 in 1950) was acquired by the Seaboard Coast Line in 1981 and was rebuilt into a 1,600 horsepower GP16 with later use on CSX Transportation and R. J. Corman Railroad before acquired by the Everett Railroad in 2002. (*Photograph by Kenneth C. Springirth*)

Below: On October 13, 2012, the Everett Railroad diesel locomotive No. 1712 is powering a passenger excursion over the former Pennsylvania Railroad trackage at Martinsburg Junction, Pennsylvania. (*Photograph by Kenneth C. Springirth*)

Above: Frederick Road in Taylor Township, Blair County, Pennsylvania is the location of Everett Railroad diesel locomotive No. 1712 powering a passenger excursion on October 13, 2012. (*Photograph by Kenneth C. Springirth*)

Right: At Martinsburg Junction, Pennsylvania, Everett Railroad diesel locomotive No. 1712 is using the wye to link up to the other end of the train for the return trip to the borough of Roaring Spring in Blair County, Pennsylvania on October 13, 2012. The Pennsylvania Railroad opened a branch line from Altoona to Roaring Spring in 1871. Currently, the Everett Railroad operates freight service from Hollidaysburg via Roaring Spring to Morrisons Cove. (*Photograph by Kenneth C. Springirth*)

Left: The Everett Railroad passenger excursion, powered by diesel locomotive No. 1712, has arrived back at the picturesque Roaring Spring, Pennsylvania passenger station on October 13, 2012. This is the only known remaining vintage railroad station in Blair County and is now owned and operated by the Roaring Spring Historical Society. (*Photograph by Kenneth C. Springirth*)

Below: On October 13, 2012, the 125th anniversary of Roaring Spring, Pennsylvania is proclaimed in the banner proudly positioned at the train station. Roaring Spring was incorporated as a borough in 1887, and the train station was built around 1905. The Pennsylvania Railroad contributed to the growth of Roaring Spring by connecting its business and industry to national markets. (*Photograph by Kenneth C. Springirth*)

Above: Vintage Pennsylvania Reading Seashore Lines type RDC-1 rail diesel car No. M-407 (built by the Budd Company in 1950) is at Cold Spring, New Jersey operating on the Cape May Seashore Lines on August 16, 1997. This line was formerly operated by the Pennsylvania–Reading Seashore Lines. Under Consolidated Rail Corporation, passenger service on the line ended in 1981 and freight service ended on October 10, 1983. New Jersey Transit acquired the tracks. (*Photograph by Kenneth C. Springirth*)

Right: Rail diesel car M-407 (one of twelve type RDC-1 cars seating 90 passengers numbered M-402 to M-413 built by the Budd Company for the Pennsylvania-Reading Seashore Lines) has arrived at the County Park and Zoo in New Jersey via the Cape May Seashore Lines on August 16, 1997. Passenger excursion service began in Cape May County in southern New Jersey between Cape May Court House and Cold Spring Village on May 18, 1996 by the Cape May Seashore Lines on trackage leased from New Jersey Transit. (*Photograph by Kenneth C. Springirth*)

Above: C. J. Tisi, past president of the Oil Creek Railway Historical Society, addresses the twenty-fifth anniversary of the Oil Creek and Titusville Railroad at the Perry Street station in Titusville, Pennsylvania on July 16, 2011. When Consolidated Rail Corporation announced plans to abandon the line from Titusville to Rouseville, the Oil Creek Railway Historical Society was formed to purchase the line, and passenger train excursion service began on July 18, 1986. (*Photograph by Kenneth C. Springirth*)

Left: Oil Creek and Titusville Railroad 1,000 horsepower type S2 diesel switcher No. 75 weighing 112 tons is crossing Franklin Street in the city of Titusville in Crawford County, Pennsylvania on July 15, 2012 on former Pennsylvania Railroad trackage. American Locomotive Company built this locomotive in 1947 for Bethlehem Steel in Lackawanna, New York. (*Photograph by Kenneth C. Springirth*)

Above: On July 14, 2012, steam locomotives Flagg Coal Company No. 75 and Viscose No. 6 are at Perry Street station in Titusville, Pennsylvania preparing to take a passenger excursion to Rynd Farm and return. This was once part of the Pennsylvania Railroad line from Pittsburgh via Titusville to Buffalo, New York. (*Photograph by Kenneth C. Springirth*)

Right: Steam locomotives No. 6 and No. 75 are on the siding at Perry Street in Titusville, Pennsylvania on July 14, 2012. Both of these locomotives were saved from the scrapper's torch and with a lot of work have been painstakingly restored. (*Photograph by Kenneth C. Springirth*)

Above: On July 15, 2012 steam locomotive No. 75 (built by Vulcan Iron Works in December 1930 as No. 2 for the Flagg Coal Company) is on the Jersey Bridge crossing Oil Creek south of Titusville, Pennsylvania with an Oil Creek and Titusville Railroad excursion on the former Pennsylvania Railroad Pittsburgh to Buffalo line. (*Photograph by Kenneth C. Springirth*)

Left: On July 15, 2012, from left to right locomotives lined up at Perry Street in Titusville on the Oil Creek and Titusville Railroad over the former Pennsylvania Railroad line are diesel switcher locomotive No. 85 (1,000 horsepower type S2 built in 1950 by the American Locomotive Company), diesel switcher locomotive No. 75 (1,000 horsepower type S2 built by American Locomotive Company in 1947), and steam locomotive No. 6 (built by Baldwin Locomotive Works in Philadelphia in November 1925). (*Photograph by Kenneth C. Springirth*)

Above: The southbound Oil Creek and Titusville Railroad excursion powered by steam locomotive No. 75 on July 15, 2012 is crossing Franklin Street in Titusville, Pennsylvania on former Pennsylvania Railroad trackage. (*Photograph by Kenneth C. Springirth*)

Right: Steam locomotive No. 75 is powering the southbound Oil Creek and Titusville Railroad excursion at Petroleum Centre in Venango County, Pennsylvania over former Pennsylvania Railroad trackage on July 15, 2012. Petroleum Centre was founded in 1866 and was largely abandoned after 1873. (*Photograph by Kenneth C. Springirth*)

Above: On October 30, 2011, speeder car No. 7821 Fairmont Rail Car model MT19-A with a Tomah cab is leading a group of speeder cars over the Jersey Bridge covering a round trip over the Oil Creek and Titusville Railroad from Titusville to Rynd Farm. A speeder car is a maintenance of way motorized vehicle once used on railroads for track inspectors and work crews. (*Photograph by Kenneth C. Springirth*)

Left: The southbound group of speeder cars on October 30, 2011 is crossing Oil Creek north of Petroleum Centre on the only Warren truss bridge on the Oil Creek and Titusville Railroad. The bridge was built by American Bridge Company in 1910. Identified by many equilateral or isosceles triangles, the Warren truss bridge was patented by James Warren and Willoughby Monzoni in 1848. (*Photograph by Kenneth C. Springirth*)

Right: A replica of Northern Central Railway steam locomotive York No. 17 with its vintage passenger cars is at New Freedom, Pennsylvania on July 12, 2013. Steam into History on June 2, 2013 began operating steam excursions over a nine-mile route between New Freedom and Hanover Junction, Pennsylvania using the new American type locomotive with a 4-4-0 wheel arrangement. New Freedom is on Pennsylvania Highway 851 just west of Interstate 83 at Exit 4 a short distance north of the state of Maryland. (*Photograph by Kenneth C. Springirth*)

Below: On July 12, 2013, at Hanover Junction in York County, Pennsylvania, steam locomotive No. 17 is in the siding to allow the Stewartstown Railroad 44 ton diesel locomotive No. 10, built by the General Electric Company, to pull the passenger cars north of the siding to allow the steam locomotive to be at the front of the train for the return trip to New Freedom. The steam locomotive was built by Kloke Locomotive Works in Elgin, Illinois headed by David Kloke. (*Photograph by Kenneth C. Springirth*)

Left: Stewartstown Railroad diesel No. 10 is moving the passenger cars north on the main line at Hanover Junction, Pennsylvania so steam locomotive No. 17 can be positioned in front of the train for the return trip to New Freedom on July 12, 2013. The Northern Central Railroad later became part of the Pennsylvania Railroad. Steam into History had about 7,000 ties replaced over the line which had not been used in years. (*Photograph by Kenneth C. Springirth*)

Below: Locomotive York No. 17 is in the borough of New Freedom, in York County, Pennsylvania on July 12, 2013. This was part of the Northern Central Railroad which was completed in 1858 connecting Baltimore, Maryland with Sunbury, Pennsylvania. In 1861, it came under control of the Pennsylvania Railroad. The original York No. 17, a domestic copy of a British "Planet" class engine, was built in 1839 by the Locks and Canals Company for the Baltimore and Susquehanna Railroad. The current No. 17 represents a standard Rogers Locomotive of the mid 1860s. While the Northern Central Railroad did not have exactly this type of locomotive, it had several other Rogers Locomotives that were used for fast passenger trains. (*Photograph by Kenneth C. Springirth*)

Right: On July 13, 2013, steam locomotive No. 17 is near Pleasant Avenue in New Freedom, Pennsylvania. On the right side of the tracks is the York County Rail Trail used by walkers and bicyclists. By the First World War, the Pennsylvania Railroad double tracked the former Northern Central Railroad line between Baltimore and Harrisburg. With the decline in freight and passenger service by the 1950s, the line was reduced to single track. Passenger service ended in 1971. (*Photograph by Kenneth C. Springirth*)

Below: The picturesque Seitzville Road crossing plays host to the Steam into History excursion on July 13, 2013. In 1972, Hurricane Agnes caused bridge damage and washout of track and Penn Central Transportation Company abandoned the railroad south of York, Pennsylvania. The Pennsylvania Department of Transportation purchased the line in 1976, and the deed was later transferred to York County. (*Photograph by Kenneth C. Springirth*)

Left: At Hanover Junction, Pennsylvania on July 13, 2013, the engineer is doing the necessary lubrication in preparation for the southbound trip to New Freedom. In 1851, this was established as a railroad junction of the Northern Central Railway and the Hanover Branch Railroad. The Northern Central Railway became part of the Pennsylvania Railroad and the Hanover Branch Railroad became part of the Western Maryland Railway, which was abandoned and rails removed by 1934. (*Photograph by Kenneth C. Springirth*)

Below: The southbound Steam into History train is south of the Hanover Junction terminus and is about to cross from North Codorus Township into Codorus Township. From Hanover Junction to the community of Railroad, the track does not veer far from Pennsylvania Highway 616. From 1996 to 2001, the surviving track was used primarily for excursion trains and under the York County Rail Trail Authority a ten-foot wide crushed stone trail was constructed on the former track bed. (*Photograph by Kenneth C. Springirth*)

Above: At the Altoona Railroaders Memorial Museum, Pennsylvania Railroad class GG1 electric locomotive No. 4913 is on display in this March 15, 2013 view. This locomotive (built in January 1942 at the Juniata Shops of the Pennsylvania Railroad) became Penn Central No. 4913 in 1968, Amtrak No. 913 in March 1973, and restored as Pennsylvania Railroad No. 4913 in June 1979. It arrived back in Altoona, Pennsylvania for display in 1980. (*Photograph by Kenneth C. Springirth*)

Right: The Railroad Museum of Pennsylvania has on display Pennsylvania Railroad class E7s Atlantic type steam locomotive with a 4-4-2 wheel arrangement No. 7002. This locomotive was originally No. 8063 built in 1902 by the Pennsylvania Railroad's Juniata Shops and was renumbered and altered to resemble No. 7002 that reportedly set a speed record of 127.1 miles per hour on June 11, 1905 near Elida, Ohio but was scrapped in 1935. The renumbered 7002 was exhibited as the world's fastest steam locomotive. (*Photograph by Kenneth C. Springirth*)

Left: Pennsylvania Railroad class B6sb switcher type steam locomotive with a 0-6-0 wheel arrangement No. 1670 is on display at the Railroad Museum of Pennsylvania. This locomotive was built at the Juniata Shops of the Pennsylvania Railroad in March 1916 and was retired in October 1957. All 238 class B6sb switchers were retrofitted with power reverse to make the frequent back and forth switching quicker and easier. (*Photograph by Kenneth C. Springirth*)

Below: Designed for rapid acceleration from frequent stops making it ideal for commuter service, the Pennsylvania Railroad class G5s ten wheeler type steam locomotive with a 4-6-0 wheel arrangement No. 5741 is displayed in this May 16, 2013 view at the Railroad Museum of Pennsylvania. This locomotive, built in November 1924 at the Juniata Shops of the Pennsylvania Railroad, was retired in December 1955. (*Photograph by Kenneth C. Springirth*)

Right: The Railroad Museum of Pennsylvania has on display Pennsylvania Railroad class B1 electric switching locomotive No. 5690. This locomotive, built in December 1934 at the Juniata Shops of the Pennsylvania Railroad, was retired in December 1971. These locomotives handled shuttling trains around Sunnyside Yard, the Penn Coach yard at Philadelphia 30th Street Station, and the Pennsylvania Railroad Harrisburg station. (*Photograph by Kenneth C. Springirth*)

Below: Pennsylvania Railroad class GG1 No. 4935, built at the Juniata Shops of the Pennsylvania Railroad in March 1943, is at the Railroad Museum of Pennsylvania. This locomotive handled Pennsylvania Railroad passenger trains in the Northeast and Keystone Corridor. It was refurbished by Amtrak with significant outside financial assistance into the Pennsylvania Railroad paint scheme of dark Brunswick green with five golden stripes and rededicated into service on May 15, 1977 and was retired in 1983. (*Photograph by Kenneth C. Springirth*)

Left: Type E7 diesel electric locomotive No. 5901, built in September 1945 for the Pennsylvania Railroad by the Electro-Motive Division of General Motors Corporation, is a wonderful sight in this May 16, 2013 view at the Railroad Museum of Pennsylvania. There were forty-six of these 2000 horsepower locomotives built for the Pennsylvania Railroad numbered 5900 to 5901 and 5840 to 5883. (*Photograph by Kenneth C. Springirth*)

Below: In this May 16, 2013 view, The Railroad Museum of Pennsylvania, located in Strasburg, Pennsylvania, has preserved Pennsylvania Railroad 4,400 horsepower class E44 electric freight locomotive No. 4465, built in July 1963 by the General Electric Company. It became Penn Central Transportation Company No. 4465 and later Amtrak No. 502. There were sixty-six of these locomotives numbered 4400 to 4465. (*Photograph by Kenneth C. Springirth*)